A Life REDEEMED

THE LIFE STORY OF Ludlow Walker

ISBN 978-1-936208-07-4
Layout and cover design: Lydia Zook
Front cover photos: istockphoto.com
Fourth printing: March 2015

Printed in the USA

For more information about Christian Aid Ministries, see page 219.

Published by:
TGS International
P.O. Box 355
Berlin, Ohio 44610 USA
Phone: 330·893·4828
Fax: 330·893·2305
www.tgsinternational.com

TGS000992

HARVEY YODER

A Life
REDEEMED

THE LIFE STORY OF Ludlow Walker

FOREWORD

Our sovereign God, who has made of one blood all nations, took note of a young Jamaican man, Ludlow Walker. God kept His hand on Ludlow as he wandered with the Merchant Marines around the globe, using that time to cultivate in him an appreciation for the many necessary disciplines of life. Eventually his adventurous spirit moved him to seek better opportunities in the small Central American country of Belize.

Our gracious God kept His protecting hand upon Ludlow all the while, pursuing him relentlessly to show him a higher plan for his life. While building a successful business and becoming mesmerized with his material pursuits, Ludlow neglected his wife and children, who eventually left him. With each new development, God seemed to be gradually closing in on him. And here, awash with success in the eyes of many worldly persons, Ludlow discovered a deep emptiness which none of his pursuits could satisfy.

You will be inspired as you read the account of how God invited him into the pursuit of spiritual life by reading the Word. He soon discovered that the Bible is alive and powerful and life-changing. God, who put the whole world together, gave him hope that He would help him put his small world together again, and He did! Spiritual growth for Ludlow was not automatic. It came only when he chose to cooperate with the in-dwelling Holy Spirit.

Ludlow pursued friendship and fellowship with the people of God in Hattieville, Belize. By them he was tutored and prepared for Kingdom life. There he was baptized and has remained faithful to those commitments ever since. He embraced a "no turning back" vow and is still moving forward in pursuit of the many other lonely souls who are without God in this world.

Being partly Jewish, of African descent, a Jamaican, a Belizean, and an American, Ludlow gives hope to people around the globe that God, who knows the hearts of all men, can put each broken life together again through surrender, redemption, and obedience. That makes one a citizen of heaven! Let God be praised for His faithfulness!

—Lester Gingerich

CONTENTS

"I WILL LOCK YOU UP"

"Ludlow, you get away from that fence! I tell you, if I catch you again trying to get over, I will tell your father! You leave those mangos alone. They don't belong to us and you know it!" Ivy Solomon Walker's voice interrupted her ten-year-old son's attempted escapade, and he dropped back down into their yard and turned an impish grin toward the kitchen window.

"Mama, I thought you were in the front yard!" Ludlow laughed.

"I am not in the yard. I am right here!" Ivy's voice was as stern as she could make it, but Ludlow knew that underneath the tone was a heart as soft and mellow as any mother's. However, as he skipped around the side of the house, brushing away a fringed palm leaf, he felt a twinge of apprehension as he recalled the reference to his father. Those words carried a sting.

John Sidney Walker was not a man who spared the rod. A police sergeant in the Jamaican capital of Kingston, he ruled his house as he ruled his precinct. He had seen too much lawlessness among the underprivileged people on the island, and he knew all too well the downward spiral of crime that began with petty misdemeanors.

No, Sergeant Walker had no tolerance for wrongdoing. His carriage was erect and he spoke with authority to all, including his family. All three of his children knew the sting of his switch, an instrument that inspired in them more fear than respect for their father. Only the threat of discipline was needed in order for them to reconsider their actions.

he had already answered any questions in his own mind before he confronted the accused. He was known to conduct his investigative work thoroughly. His suspicions rarely went unsubstantiated, were someone to investigate further.

Ludlow, who at ten years old was getting to be almost as tall as his father, tried to meet his father's gaze. His eyes took in the way his father's firm chin moved as he spoke with careful deliberation.

The Jamaican features of his father had been passed on to his children, but his dark skin color had been diluted and all three children were lighter in color. Their maternal grandfather, a Jew, had passed his genes on to the third generation, and the children reflected their mother's mixed heritage.

"Stealing, even if it is only fruit, is a crime." His father's voice jerked Ludlow back into the present and away from his observations about skin color. He noticed the tiny wrinkles on each side of his father's almost black eyes. They were not smile wrinkles, like the old woman he bought his sweets from. No, the tiny lines on his father's face could hardly be that.

"The Clemsons' yard is private property."

No longer could Ludlow allow his mind to daydream. Incriminating evidence was piling up for the inevitable, but like a cautious and deliberate judge, John Walker did not hurry. "Not only have you stolen, you have trespassed on their property."

"But they are our landlords. We rent this house from them." Even to his own young mind, the excuse sounded lame, but Ludlow felt obliged to put up a defense.

Ignoring Ludlow's desperate attempt to excuse his actions, his father continued relentlessly. "Not only have I warned you repeatedly about the consequences of going into their yard and stealing, but I have also punished you many times."

There was no denying that fact. Ludlow felt the skin twitch on the back of his legs. Yes, there had been many warnings.

"Still, you have not stopped. Mama says you climbed the fence again today. You stole fruit. You trespassed. You disobeyed." One by one, the charges were laid out.

Ludlow shifted his slight weight from one foot to the other. This was always the hard part; the long, agonizing ritual of having his sins enumerated one by one in vivid and unvarnished detail.

For Ludlow, it would have been easier to take if his father had simply meted out the punishment he deserved and gotten it over with. Most certainly, the whippings he had gotten the other times had not been easy or light, for no sergeant would risk appearing soft even to his own family. Afterwards, however, Ludlow could rest easier, knowing the punishment was now over even if the pain might persist for several days.

"You are being a bad example to Gerald and Joy." His father's relentless voice went on.

"But they eat the fruit I bring!" A wild hope sprang up in Ludlow's heart. "They like the mangos and papayas too!"

A long, silent stare was the only response to Ludlow's passionate words. Then the list of crimes continued. "Your mother forbids you to go over there and get fruit. You disobey your mother. I forbid you. You disobey me. You bribe your siblings with fruit to buy their silence. You ingratiate yourself with the Clemsons' gardener so he won't report you."

They were alone in the bedroom that Ludlow normally shared with Gerald. The delectable smells of dinner cooking in the kitchen drifted into the little bedroom. Smells of a dinner that Ludlow knew from past experiences he would not be sharing. He could hear Joy's voice outside through the open window.

His father's head was silhouetted in front of the window. The light clearly shone on his short-cropped black hair. The final evidence was given, the sentence pronounced. The belt slid easily from around the waist of John Walker and unrolled to its full length.

The ripe mango slipped easily off the stem that dangled from the tree limb. Ludlow knew it was ripe because his fingers left soft indentations on the skin of the yellowing fruit.

He liked this tree. The spreading branches grew horizontally as if designed for climbing. Not that any other trees with different growth patterns were difficult for him to conquer. His tree-climbing abilities made almost any fruit easily accessible, but this mango tree was especially nice. The fruit was as rewarding to his taste buds as he had imagined it would be.

It had been easy today to get over the wall and into the forbidden garden. His mother had taken the two younger children into the city to get shoes for school. The chores that his mother had left for him could easily be done in half an hour, he thought. Barely waiting until they were out of sight, he had scaled the fence and picked out his favorite tree.

Ludlow always admired this tropical grove. There were so many trees and such an abundance of fruit. Although they had plenty of mangos at his house, there was something so much more thrilling in harvesting and enjoying his own delectable choices. "They never use all the mangos," he had told his mother more than once. "They just lie rotting on the ground."

In spite of the frequent beatings (Ludlow rubbed his seat in remembrance), there was just something about the adventure, the daring, the thrill of seeing if he could pull off his escapades that made him do it again and again.

Once he had heard his mother ask, "John, why don't you just talk to the Clemsons and see if they mind if Ludlow gets the fruit?" The low, emphatic answer Ludlow heard was clearly a no. But it had given him new excuses to talk to that little voice that kept warning him about continuing his raids.

The hot sun was penetrating the interior of the mango tree where Ludlow now perched enjoying his fruit. Should he take some back for a peace offering in case his siblings questioned him? So far, that tactic had always worked and their own sticky lips sealed their silence.

A branch was irritating his bare leg. As he bent over to break the offending twig, he suddenly realized he was no longer alone. People don't look the same when you view them from above, looking down on top of their heads. They appear much shorter and somewhat out of proportion, their heads bigger and their feet smaller. But in spite of that, Ludlow had no problem recognizing the figure looking silently up at him from below the mango tree. It was his father.

A wave of heat swept over him and young Ludlow broke into a sweat. The partially eaten mango dropped from his hand, bounced through the limbs, and splattered onto the ground below. Ludlow gripped the tree trunk with trembling hands while John Walker silently continued his measured staring through the branches at his son.

There was silence in the grove and the air was heavy with expectation as though a storm was brewing. Maybe they would have a hurricane. That might be why his father had come home unexpectedly in the middle of the day. Maybe it was to warn them and help them prepare for the devastating winds and rain that frequently swept across Jamaica. Ludlow's thoughts were frantically groping for anything that made sense.

But the figure below the tree remained as silent as the air about him. Finally John Walker bent over, picked up a bruised mango, and inspected it. Still he said nothing to the boy trapped in the tree above him.

Ludlow waited. This encounter was unlike any he had experienced before. Usually he was told what to do. This time there was no direct order, no words. Just a heavy silence.

Should he stay in the tree and outwait his father? Should he climb down and get his punishment over with? Would his father eventually climb up after him if he stayed there?

Ludlow looked up. There were still branches above him and he could go higher, farther away from the silent figure below him. Ludlow looked down again. His father was now leaning comfortably against the tree trunk, one leg bent at an angle as he propped his foot against the tree.

Waiting. That was always the hardest for Ludlow. The usual lectures were hard because he had to wait for the punishment. He always wanted to get the penalty over with. It was easier on his nature to plummet to the bottom of the hole he had dug for himself. Then, even if it took awhile for him to climb back out, at least he was going back up to life as usual.

He shifted on the branch he was sitting on; then, lithe as a leopard, he swung himself from limb to limb and dropped to the ground in front of the silent figure. His father's eyes bored straight into Ludlow's eyes, and for a brief moment the boy felt that his entire mind and heart were exposed to the penetrating gaze.

"Come with me." The two set out toward their house. With only slightly more effort than his son, John Walker pulled himself onto the wall and dropped beside Ludlow inside their own yard. Briskly, Ludlow's father brushed the dust from his uniform, and with a quick nod toward his son, he set off down the street.

Kingston is a fascinating city, even to its residents, and Ludlow always enjoyed the bustling sidewalks filled with people, the vehicles passing by on the road, and the camaraderie of the diverse culture that made the city a unique place. But today, there was no time to enjoy his native city. He easily kept step with his father's brisk steps, but inside, he was apprehensive about his father's intentions. Obviously there was to be something different this time, although Ludlow was quite sure it was not going to be anything easier.

Several people respectfully greeted the police sergeant, nodding to John Walker. In response, Ludlow's father either nodded briefly or spoke a few words. Several of the neighbors glanced inquisitively at Ludlow, but it was not unusual for a man to take a walk with his son. From the look on the officer's face, though, his acquaintances discerned that this was no time for small talk. There was a certain look in the sergeant's eyes that did not bode well for someone.

Ludlow had often been at his father's place of work. The police headquarters were situated right on the main thoroughfare, set back from the street, and had an iron railing around the front yard.

The door leading into the station stood open to allow any cooling breezes to sweep through the massive hall. Through this open door and straight down the hall the two marched. John Walker had now taken hold of his son's arm, and when they reached the end of the hall, they turned left and walked through a narrow corridor. The place seemed empty. Their footsteps echoed on the hard floor in perfect tempo with Ludlow's beating heart.

This was where—no, his father wouldn't! This was the jail! Where the town drunks and miscreants were locked up! No! He wouldn't!

But he did.

The iron-barred door to the empty cell was not locked. Sergeant Walker pulled the door open with one hand, and stepping inside, he pulled his son in after him. He closed the door and stood for a moment, looking at Ludlow's wide eyes. "I will lock you up," he stated in that same stiff and stern tone he reserved for correcting Ludlow. "I have whipped you. I have talked to you. I have done everything I know to make you quit stealing fruit from the Clemsons' yard, and yet you persist."

Abruptly releasing Ludlow's arm, John Walker opened the cell door, stepped into the corridor, and swung the door shut. Taking a key from the ring on his belt, he locked the cell. He stood for only a brief second, looking through the bars at his son, and then he turned and walked away, the sound of his boots echoing harshly through the building.

The young boy's eyes darted around the lock-up as they gradually adjusted to the dim light. He was horrified at what he saw. A single iron cot with a metal spring mesh was the only piece of furniture in the cell. The walls were unpainted gray concrete. A small window high up on the wall was covered with heavy bars. Ludlow knew immediately that even without bars, the window would have been too small for his slight body to slip through.

Ludlow opened his mouth and breathed heavily as though he had been running. His stomach churned, wanting to rid itself of the offensive mango. The smell of the place penetrated his senses, and as he sifted through the mingled odors of stale sweat, urine, and the unmistakable stench of human waste, he cringed and tried to ignore the bucket in the corner.

At first Ludlow's thoughts had no pattern. There was just a general panic along with trying to make sense of what had happened to him. Why was he here? What had he done that would cause his father to do something this drastic to his own son?

Jail did not seem in any way connected to mangos or papayas or even to scaling the concrete wall and climbing into the yard next door. Grasping the bars with both hands, Ludlow looked across the narrow hall to the bland concrete wall opposite him. He twisted his head to see what was to his right and to his left.

Even though he had eaten the mango, his stomach growled. He was to have had lunch after his mother returned. Not that Ludlow actually felt like eating, but his young body involuntarily announced mealtimes with clockwork precision.

His mother. The thought of Ivy Solomon Walker brought a sting to his eyes. Did she know where he was? Did Gerald and Joy know their brother was in jail? What about his schoolmates? Would they find out? The people from church? Now his thoughts began to churn in dizzying circles, running around and around his incarceration and the impending consequences.

How long would his father keep him locked up? Would he have to stay here overnight? Ludlow looked at the patch of blue sky in the cell window and tried to imagine it turning black with the coming of night. Panic began to constrict his throat. He pushed against the hard, cold, unyielding bars. He wanted to cry out, to scream at his father and beg for release from this terrible place. He could feel his heart pounding wildly in his chest. Waves of nausea threatened to send him to the bucket, but Ludlow kept swallowing the bile that crept upward in his throat.

He tried to still himself so he could listen more closely for footsteps, footsteps of his father that would mean deliverance. Or would he merely stop, look through the bars, and then walk away? The thought brought a fresh attack of panic to the young thief.

He could hear moans from further down the hall. Probably they came from some drunk trying to recover after a night's binge in town.

The Walker children knew about the people who spent time in jail. Their father spoke disdainfully of the scum who kept the officers busy dragging their intoxicated bodies into the police van and dumping them into cells. He spoke of their shiftless habits and their inability to keep jobs. He also told his family about the thieves who seemed destined to end up locked away for years because their misdemeanors turned into greater crimes. They were addicted to stealing, those thieves were.

Thieves like Ludlow. Yes, his father had told him bluntly that he was a thief. He had been one for a long time, stealing fruit. Although his father had told him often enough, Ludlow had never really accepted that fact. Oh yes, he knew that he stole. But that was just fruit. He was not a thief like the burglars who broke into people's houses and took valuables.

Ludlow looked around the cell once more. He was in jail. He really was a criminal. That fact riveted itself into his young mind with startling clarity. He was no different from any other thief. He took what was forbidden. He robbed someone else's possessions.

He knew other boys stole too. They took bigger stuff than he ever did. Some of the boys in school even bragged about goods they took from market stalls or from relatives' houses. Of course, Ludlow was not that kind of thief. Or was he?

Now he had time for reflection. A persistent voice was speaking in his heart and the voice was right. He had often been tempted to steal merchandise from the market stalls. He had watched to see if the sharp-eyed stall keepers noticed him. But he had never taken anything. Not yet.

Ludlow began to sob. Not angry, uncontrolled crying, but just the crying that goes with feeling forsaken and unloved. He wept as he acknowledged that his father was right about him. He was a thief, and now he was facing the same consequences other thieves faced.

"Come out." The words were no kinder than usual, no more sympathetic than John Walker normally used, but to Ludlow, they were the most welcome words he had ever heard in his life.

He marveled that the sun was still shining, and he drew in deep breaths on his way home through the city streets. His feet would not go slowly; he began to run.

It had been no more than two hours that the young boy had been locked up, but for Ludlow it had been a span of time that could not be measured by any clock. Although he did not know it, he had begun the long journey of becoming a man while he had been in that cell. For the first time in his memory, he was beginning to see a relationship between his actions and the consequences that followed.

Upon arriving home, Ludlow hugged his mother deliriously and played with his siblings, but without his usual cockiness. Although all seemed normal at home, something was different. While unable to explain his feelings out loud, he somehow knew he had changed. Although John and Ivy Walker saw the change in their son, they still watched him closely. Would Ludlow revert to his old habits with time?

One day soon after his jail experience, Ludlow caught himself staring at the ripe mangos hanging in clear sight on the other side of the wall. He felt the old familiar watering in his mouth as he thought of the delicious taste of the sun-ripened, stolen fruit. All he had to do was scale the fence, grab it, and be right back.

But as quickly as the thought entered his head, his mind took him back to the hours he had spent in the jail cell. The horrible feeling he had experienced came back to him with startling clarity.

"Just keep your old mangos!" Ludlow shouted to the tree. Then he laughed at himself. He turned and galloped around the side of the house, beating his stick against the concrete wall all the way.

CHAPTER 2

RECOGNITION AND REWARDS

"Line up! Attention!" The Jamaican Cadet Force officer's voice rang out with authority, and the thirty-some teenage boys stood tall, shoulders back, looking straight ahead with rigid attention showing in every line of their bodies.

The officer walked down the front of the line, inspecting the troops. Ludlow stood tall in his place, letting his eyes take in the swaying palm trees separating them from the ocean. The white sands of the beach in front of them stood out in contrast to the deep Caribbean turquoise of the water that surrounded this small island.

"Saunders!" The bark of the officer's voice broke sharply into the quietness of the morning. "Step forward."

"Yes, sir!" Saunders' reply was high-pitched. His voice had not yet deepened.

Without moving his head, Ludlow nevertheless looked sideways as far as his eyeballs could roll in their sockets. He saw Tim step forward.

"When you are in training, what are you in training for?" The challenge came with scorn. "Do you expect to gain any recognition with shoes looking like that?"

Oh, no. Tim's shoes must not be polished according to the officer's standards. Ludlow desperately wanted to check his own polished, black, laced-up boots, but he knew better than to look. If he could somehow rub the tops of his shoes against the back of his trouser legs, he would feel more comfortable, but it was too late to try that now. He curled his toes nervously inside his shoes.

"When we recruit members, we are not recruiting babies. We want men! Do you understand that?"

"Yes, sir!" Tim's tremulous voice squeaked. Tim was only fifteen, a year older than Ludlow, but he was shorter by a good number of inches and seemed to be maturing late. Ludlow felt a surge of pity for his friend as the officer berated him in front of all the cadets.

"I will give you thirty minutes to return to camp, shine your shoes until I am satisfied, and then report to my tent. I refuse to include slobs in my division. You will be given late kitchen duty for a week, and no off-island privileges."

No off-island privileges! Kitchen duty! Ludlow stiffened his spine and stared straight ahead.

The small island where their camp was located was ideal for the fourteen- to seventeen-year-old boys who were in military-like training. Sandy beaches, lots of space for military drills, and tall palm trees to shade the tents from the hot tropical sun made for ideal surroundings for the youngsters. However, all of them looked forward to the evenings when they were allowed to go by boat to the mainland and walk around town in their uniforms, feeling dignified and grown-up as the townspeople admired them and treated them with respect. Besides, on the main island of Jamaica there was always good food to eat as opposed to the amateur offerings of the young camp cooks.

Ludlow heard Tim stumble away. The officer continued his inspection. Ludlow held himself as erect as he knew how and trusted that his earlier efforts at shoe polishing would pass. He despised the monotony of that tedious task, but now he was glad for every minute he had spent polishing his footwear.

The officer was only slightly taller than Ludlow, and the young boy held himself immobile as he was inspected. When the officer finally passed on, Ludlow exhaled and realized he had been holding his breath.

He enjoyed being a part of the disciplined group of trainees. He felt he was part of something worthwhile. His young heart raced with exhilaration when they went through the rigorous military training every day, racing across the sand in relays and doing sit-ups, knee bends, pull-ups, and chin-ups.

"Do you think you could swim to the main island?" Lance asked curiously, sitting comfortably on the sandy beach. The embers of the campfire glowed in the darkness. The group of five boys sat around in relaxation, gazing at the fire. The flames flickered and illuminated their faces, picking up their features in the black night.

"I could," Theodore said stoutly. "It only takes a few minutes to row by boat, and I know I could swim that short distance."

The boys gazed across the water to the lights of the town. They could see the Catholic cathedral spire, illuminated by lights. The stained glass windows sparkled like faint jewels in the distance.

"Anyone ever been inside the Catholic church?" Lance asked.

"No!" Ludlow's response was emphatic. "I heard they have all kinds of candles and statues there. They worship idols."

"Our church is the best church ever," Herbert said with fervor. "We have all the dignitaries and important people in our church."

"That's not the only reason we have the best church," Ludlow added quickly. "The Anglican church is recognized by our government as the official religion just as it is in England."

"Long live the Queen!" the boys all chorused together.

"You know we won't be part of Great Britain much longer," Lance reminded them. "When we gain independence, we will be our own country with our own government."

"We'll still be Anglicans. Did you see Bishop Percival Gibson last Sunday? I am proud to have our own Jamaican bishop," Ludlow remembered. "We will soon be completely capable of running our own country. Long live Jamaica!" The boys all sprang to their feet and held their hands to their foreheads, saluting each other.

Herbert stood beside Ludlow, his dark features serious with the moment. Ludlow reached out in the darkness and tickled Herbert's ear.

Herbert turned his head slowly, and then with a yell, he leaped on Ludlow. The two boys fell to the sand, laughing and wrestling each other good-naturedly. The others joined in and the night air rang with their youthful shouts, but when the curfew whistle sounded, they immediately became cadets again and sprinted for their tents.

"I'm home," Ludlow called, trying to make his voice sound as deep as his father's.

"Oh, son! Welcome back." Ivy turned from the kitchen sink to face Ludlow. She reached welcoming arms toward her oldest son.

Ludlow remained standing stiffly as though he were still in the cadets' camp. His uniform was exactly right, his brass buttons gleamed, his shoes were polished to perfection, and his cap tilted to the left just enough to give him a slight rakish appearance without violating regulations.

"My, what a fine young man you are," Ivy said as she realized Ludlow wanted her to admire him. Ludlow stood still in expectancy. When would she notice?

"Do you want something to eat?" His mother's mind went to practical matters. Ludlow exhaled silently and rolled his eyes as he had seen senior officers do when they were frustrated with a slow response.

"Mom! Don't you see?" Ludlow said impatiently. "Look!"

Ivy looked where Ludlow pointed. She saw a stripe on his shoulder, the yellow shining brightly against the khaki background. "You got an award or something?"

"I was promoted! Mom, I am a lance corporal! I passed the written exam with honors! It is hard to achieve this distinction. I am one of only ten boys who won this promotion!"

"That's good, son. I am sure you did well. When did you last eat?"

Ludlow shook his head. His mother did not understand. She did not realize how difficult it had been for him to maintain perfect behavior, to achieve the high marks on his written exam, and to display the character traits necessary to be recognized by the men who ran the camp. Those officers were professional military men, and they were tough with all the boys.

"I have cooked rice for dinner tonight, but I am sure you are hungry right now. I will fix a plate for you. In another two hours your father will come home from work and Gerald and Joy should be home from their classes."

"I *was* hungry," Ludlow admitted as he ate his mother's good cooking again. Even if she did not understand what he had achieved, she certainly knew how to fill his stomach with what every growing boy needs—good food!

"Good work, son."

Ludlow smiled back at his father.

For a long moment, the two stood eye to eye. Ludlow's heart beat faster as he realized how rare were the words his father had just spoken.

John Sidney Walker was a police sergeant first. That was his job, his career, and he would not let anyone forget that. He was a husband second and a father to his children third. The entire family knew that.

For the first time in his life, Ludlow felt warmth for his father creep into his heart. Before, John Walker was an important figure in his life and a strict disciplinarian who provided well for his family. But now, as he heard the note of pride in his father's voice, Ludlow knew him as a father.

John Walker's eyes drifted to the yellow stripe once again. He smiled. "After dinner I want you to go with me. We will visit some friends."

The warmth in Ludlow's heart spread. His father was proud of him. He wanted to show him off to his friends! Ludlow wanted to shout—to jump with glee. He had finally proven himself to be someone! His father had noticed him.

"Ludlow is now a lance corporal," John Walker said again and again that evening as he took his tall son with him to visit his fellow police officers and friends. The men smiled and nodded and congratulated both father and son.

"One of the greatest regrets in my career is that I never advanced beyond the rank of a sergeant. I have worked long and hard to advance, but there were always other men ahead of me." Ludlow could hear the tone of defeat in his father's voice and realized how much his achievement meant to his father. Even though his own promotion was minor in comparison to his father's adult position, he felt he was now being treated as an equal. He held himself proudly erect as they walked the sidewalks of Kingston together.

Achievement. Recognition. Significance—this was what his heart had been longing for, and to finally taste it was sweet indeed.

"Son, you continue to work hard and you will advance. No matter how hard it is, do not give up or even slack off for one minute. Our island will someday soon take its place among the nations of the world, and you can be one of the leaders. Your future is before you, and I want you to advance as far as possible."

Ludlow felt as proud as he had ever felt. Not only had he been promoted to the rank of lance corporal in the Jamaican Cadet Force, but now he had gained his father's approval as well. The future looked extremely bright to him right then.

"O Lord, we sing of the magnificent works you have created," Ludlow sang with the rest of the choir.

Church on Sunday was as expected as school on weekdays. The Walker family attended regularly, careful to take their places among the people of society on the island. Early on, Ludlow and Gerald had joined the acolytes, singing in the choir and joining the Sunday morning processions as the church officials filed down the aisle toward the front and led in the formal services.

For years Ludlow had attended church. Like school, sometimes he enjoyed it and other times he wished he could escape and spend his time pursuing other activities outdoors. But now, standing in a back row with the other teenagers, he was glad to be here. He looked at Marguerite standing in the row ahead of him and admired the pleasing contrast of the white collar against her dark skin. Even though they were all dressed in the choir robes of the Anglican Church, he still appreciated the touch of femininity that escaped the rather formal attire of the girls.

Theodore nudged him sharply. Ludlow closed his mouth and frowned.

What did Theodore want now? Probably Ludlow was off tune again. Even though he had sung in the choir for years, he occasionally let his voice drift into a monotone that aggravated the choir director and the more musically gifted choir members. He tried to concentrate on the music, but his eyes kept drifting to Marguerite.

Going to an all boys' school meant that Ludlow rarely had a chance to see girls or interact with them. Even in the evenings they were not allowed to do much socializing. But in church the boys and girls stood in close proximity, which was exciting to young Ludlow.

Moving his hand slowly, Ludlow reached forward and pulled gently on the back of Marguerite's robe. Not much, just enough to let her know he was standing right behind her. A slight movement of the girl's head gave Ludlow immense satisfaction. She had acknowledged him! His heart skipped.

Later, sitting on the men's side of the church, Ludlow glanced across the aisle to where the girls sat. Yes, there she was, her profile a pleasing composition as she gazed at the minister reading the lesson. Then, as though she sensed he was watching her, she slowly turned her head enough to look at the boys' section. When her eyes met his gaze, a slight smile spread across her face and then she looked forward again.

That was enough for Ludlow. No words needed to be spoken, no notes needed to be passed between the two. To have encouraging responses from Marguerite was enough to last Ludlow until the next Sunday.

"Good day! I hope you have a wonderful Sunday," Ludlow said politely to the group of girls that came down the church steps into the bright sunshine. Some of the girls giggled, but Marguerite gently nodded in his direction and once more gave Ludlow a smile that warmed his heart.

CHAPTER 3

THE LURE OF THE SEA

The list on the paper looked endless. Sitting in his desk chair, Ludlow could see through the open window of the auto parts store where he worked as a clerk. Customers coming in stated their needs and the salesmen brought their parts to the counter.

It looks livelier out there, Ludlow thought. *At least I could talk to people instead of checking over the seemingly endless list of items to inventory.*

"Thirty-nine O-rings minus twenty-three would leave sixteen in stock. Time to reorder," Ludlow spoke out loud. He made a check mark on the order sheet. Then he ran his finger down the accounting sheet until he found another item to update.

High school behind him, Ludlow had been pleased when he was hired at the parts store. The pay was reasonably good and the working conditions pleasant enough. He had especially enjoyed the initial challenge of learning the business, but as he became familiar with the accounting practices, the same steady routine became boring to the energetic nineteen-year-old. "Just lists of parts and numbers," he complained to his mother. "I get restless and want to do something exciting."

"Like what?" Ivy wanted to know. She could see the restless energy pulsing in her tall young son.

"I wish I knew. Maybe something off the island. I have always wanted to travel."

Gerald looked up from his book. "I travel by reading."

"Books! I am done with books!" Ludlow exclaimed. "I want to do something with my muscles—something exciting," he reiterated.

"You know we are proud that you have a job," his mother reminded him. "Most students find it hard to get a job after they leave school. Especially one that pays well."

"Money isn't everything," Ludlow retorted. "Besides, I can never advance much in that store. Even the clerks don't earn much more than I do. I don't want to waste the rest of my life growing old and moldy over endless lists." Ludlow flexed his long arms above his head and touched the ceiling with ease.

One day as he bent over his lists in the office, Ludlow heard a commotion at the front door. "Ahoy, mateys," a strong voice came roaring through the door. "Landside again and needing parts for our ship motors."

Ludlow stared out the open window into the store. A sailor!

"Where did you return from this time, Sammy?" one of the clerks asked.

"South America. Way down off the coast of Argentina. Now that is some country, I tell you. Speak Spanish, they do. Big city with lots of activities, if you know what I mean." He winked and laughed boisterously.

Ludlow knew his father's contempt of sailors. John Walker routinely arrested drunken, brawling sailors and locked them up. When a ship came to dock in their harbor and the sailors came ashore, many of them tried to make up for the monotonous weeks or even months they had spent at sea. Like stabled horses let out to pasture, they descended eagerly upon the town's trouble spots and were the bane of the police forces. In spite of that, Ludlow found himself listening in fascination as Sammy spoke of the wonders of seaports he had visited.

"That's what I want to do," Ludlow told himself excitedly, his pulse racing as he zeroed in on the restlessness stirring inside him. "I want to become a sailor. It sounds like good pay, adventure, and an opportunity to see the world, all in one!"

The next time Sammy came into the auto parts store, Ludlow left his desk and went out behind the counter. He followed the colorful sailor out the door. "Sir! How does one go about getting on board a ship? I mean, to work on a ship and become a sailor?" Ludlow asked hastily.

Sammy looked at the youth. He smiled. "You got the bug, have you?" he chuckled. "Many a young man thinks he wants to go to sea. How old are you?"

"Nineteen."

Sammy nodded. "That's old enough." He squinted in the bright sun as he looked up at Ludlow. "You got to have a passport. Also helps to know someone on board like a captain, or have a relative on board."

Ludlow felt his hopes begin to plunge. No one in his family had seafaring connections. He did not know any captains.

"Oh, not everyone has to do it that way," Sammy assured him, sensing the youth's disappointment. "Many a man has started with nothing. Ships' captains are hiring all the time, but it is hard labor and you have to work your way up slowly."

"I can work hard," Ludlow said. "I'm not afraid of work."

Taking hold of Ludlow's arm, Sammy felt the young man's muscles. "I can see you are strong. But can you work hard for long periods of time? Many men begin on ships and leave again after the first voyage. It is not the life for everyone."

"I could do it," Ludlow insisted.

With money carefully saved from his job, Ludlow applied for a passport. He had it shipped to his work address so his parents would not know about it—especially his father. But he could not resist telling his mother.

"I am going to see if I can get work on board a ship. I have my passport!"

"Oh, Ludlow!" Ivy protested. "What will your father say?"

"He won't know it," Ludlow said simply. "He won't know it till I'm gone."

There was a moment of silence as Ivy looked into her son's face. A man, that was what Ludlow was. John Walker had a hard time accepting that fact. He still wanted to keep his son completely under his control. Too often, if there was a conflict between father and son, Ivy had to stand silently by and hope their storms would blow over. No, she would not tell her husband what Ludlow was up to. She did not want any more tumultuous arguments.

"Captain Kirkland?" Ludlow addressed the man obviously in command of the ship at the harbor.

"Yes?"

"I heard you are hiring people to chip and repaint your ship. I would like to apply for the job." Ludlow stood straight and tall.

The captain scrutinized the youth critically. "Have you any experience?"

"Oh, yes," Ludlow lied confidently. "I am quite capable of doing the job."

Experienced though he was in detecting dishonesty, the captain obviously liked Ludlow enough to say, "Well, I hope so. Report to work tomorrow morning."

It was that easy to get on board a ship. True, he was not a sailor, and yet Ludlow felt convinced that even to work as a day laborer on board might be a way to get closer to his dream.

"We'll do the stern first," Arnold, the foreman, told him the next morning.

Stern. Ludlow looked inquiringly at the wide deck of the cargo ship. What exactly was the stern?

"Have you never been on board a ship before?" Arnold guessed shrewdly.

"Umm," Ludlow began, trying to stall for time.

Arnold laughed. "Don't try to fool me. Look, sailors use a language all their own. If you want to work on a ship, you absolutely have to learn that language. Stern," he repeated, "is the back of the ship. Bow is the front. Then there is the poop deck down under and the galley for starters." As he spoke, Arnold waved in the general direction of the places on board as he named them.

"Oh, yeah, I know," Ludlow stammered.

"No, you don't," Arnold retorted good-naturedly. "I know a rookie when I see one, and you are one! Sometimes you can cover your ignorance by bluffing, but not always. I see I will need to teach you everything."

The two became friends as they worked side by side for the next several weeks. Arnold had sailed on this ship for three years. It was nothing really exciting, only transporting coarse salt from the Turks and Caicos Islands back to Kingston, but to Ludlow that sounded exciting enough. A sailor, sailing the open seas!

"Walker, I cannot hire you. I have openings for only experienced sailors who can take their turn to steer the ship," Captain Kirkland said as he faced the unhappy boy.

A feeling of desperation swept over Ludlow. "Please, sir! I am sure I could learn very quickly!"

"No." The answer was final. "I can hire only experienced deckhands for this trip."

Ludlow felt his hopes fade. He was becoming desperate. His father was sure to find out eventually that he had quit his job at the auto parts store three weeks earlier. He still went home at nights, and although his mother knew where he was and what he was doing, he had managed to keep his secret from the rest of the family.

"Then, sir, could you please write a letter of recommendation to help me get a job on board another ship?"

"Ah, sure!" Captain Kirkland seemed eager for a chance to get rid of this persistent young man by obliging this request. He reached for a notebook, scribbled a quick message, and handed it to Ludlow.

Ludlow clutched the letter and studied it carefully. The captain had scrawled on a piece of his letterhead that one, Ludlow Walker, had provided adequate service to the captain and he was recommending the young man to anyone who might be interested in taking him on board a ship. It did not specify what kind of experience Ludlow had; it simply stated that he had provided adequate services.

"Thank you, Captain," Ludlow said gratefully. He carefully folded the letter, placed it in his pocket, and left the ship.

"You can either give away this stack of books or let Gerald and Joy have them," Ludlow told his mother carelessly.

"Are you sure you are doing the right thing?" Ivy's face was lined with concern.

"Mom, I am absolutely not going back to the parts store. They probably wouldn't give my job back anyway. No, I must try to get a job on a ship. I want to get away from the island."

"Take this with you," Ivy said, placing a black Bible on top of the stack of clothes her son had positioned on his bed.

"I told you I won't need my textbooks anymore," Ludlow protested as he put the Bible back on top of his used schoolbooks.

"The Bible is not just a textbook. This is God's Word and you need it," his mother urged.

Ludlow smiled at her. "As far as I'm concerned, the Bible is just another textbook. It's just a collection of stories that may or may not be true."

"Surely your teachers taught you better than that! You were instructed in chapel about God and the Bible. You know it is more than a textbook!" Ivy was distressed at her son's flippant attitude toward the Holy Book.

"I think God has retired," Ludlow said seriously. "I do believe He created the world at some time, but now we have science that teaches us how to live, and the more educated we become, the less we need God."

His thoughts flitted back to his religious education. All the Bible memory work, the religious lessons read by the teachers, the boring sermons he heard in church—they all seemed to be a distant part of his childhood.

"Even the religious leaders of church are simply distant figures, like the Queen in England. God is like that too. He's remote, busy with difficult things, and not interested in me. I have to make my own life. What I want is money," Ludlow said bluntly. "Money and excitement and travel. I want to see what the world can offer."

Putting his clothes into his backpack, he nodded toward the books. "Someday someone may need those, but it won't be me."

Silent tears streamed down Ivy Walker's cheeks as she kissed her son goodbye. Ludlow was so sure of himself, so confident. "Lord, watch over him," she prayed.

Karl Scemedan. The name of the Scandinavian ship was painted in bold letters close to the bow. Ludlow felt his heart beat faster as he surveyed the giant cargo ship.

Reynolds Company. That was the corporation that was exporting bauxite ore from Jamaica and hauling it to the United States of America.

Yes, they needed men. "Able-bodied seamen" was the term. Seamen who knew their way around the ship, knew about the divided watches that were marked by the ship's bells, and most importantly, knew how to steer. Ludlow knew that steering was an important skill—one he did not possess.

The line of applicants in front of him moved slowly. He looked ahead to where Captain Stevenson was interviewing the hopefuls. What would the captain say to an inexperienced lad like Ludlow?

"Your first time?" the man behind him spoke.

Ludlow turned to face the speaker. "Oh, I've worked on a ship before," he replied quickly.

"Good. I'm Jackson." The man reached out a friendly hand.

"And you? Have you sailed before?" Ludlow tried nervously to turn the attention away from himself.

"Three years, mostly for Reynolds. They're a good company to work for. Hard work but good pay."

Ludlow nodded. He wanted to ask Jackson why he had quit.

"Dismissed for drunkenness," Jackson said easily, as though reading his mind. "Bad stuff, that drink. Hard to stay away from, though, once you hit shore and have money in your wallet. Do you drink?"

Ludlow shook his head. "No."

"Then you should do well at this job." Looking at the line ahead of him, Jackson shook his head. "Lots of men trying to get a job, though. Doesn't look good for us."

The two stood side by side, watching the vessel sail. Sailing without them. By the time they had been interviewed, it was evident that the captain already had a full crew.

"Stay on the dock and I will call you if I can use you," he had said over and over again. So Ludlow had stayed, along with Jackson.

Now the young man toyed only briefly with the idea of going to a motel. Motels would cost money. Ludlow had only a few British pounds he had saved up from his jobs, and he had no idea how long it would be before he would earn any more wages. The ship pulling farther and farther away from the harbor seemed to symbolize his shrinking options.

"Hey, you got a place for the night?" Jackson's voice interrupted his reverie. "Come along home with me. You can stay at our house."

"This is my mother . . . my sisters." Jackson introduced Ludlow to his family.

Ludlow shook hands and greeted the women respectfully. There was no mention of a husband or father, and he refrained from asking questions. Although he had passed many homes of the poor on the island, Ludlow's visit to Jackson's house was his first personal encounter with poverty on this level. Although the little house was clean, it was obvious that the family lived very frugally.

"Eat with us," the girls invited him. "We have plenty."

Ludlow ate the savory rice offered to him. He enjoyed the company of the girls, and Jackson was pleasant and jovial. Ludlow could not imagine him actually being drunk.

"Yes, stay with us until you find a job," the women urged after Jackson explained how they had met. "We do not have much, but you are welcome." Ludlow was happy to accept. His meager funds would now last much longer.

"Tomorrow we go to Saint Ann's Bay. The Reynolds Company is there also and we will try our luck there," Jackson told his new friend. "We can go by bus. It is only seven miles. But right now it's time to get some sleep."

Lying in the dark beside his sleeping friend, Ludlow felt the first feelings of apprehension about his future begin to grow. Right now his former job seemed quite appealing. When could he get a job on a ship? Would it be any easier in Saint Ann's? How much longer would his money last?

Turning over, Ludlow stared into the darkness. Next door a radio played loudly, while a dog barked incessantly in the distance.

Ludlow wondered what was going on at home. How would John Walker react to his son abandoning a secure job and running off to sea? Would he treat his wife with stony silence—or with something worse—for not telling him what she knew?

Would Gerald and Joy miss him? Although their lives had gone different ways as they each became involved in their school activities, they were still family. Already he missed his younger sister's cheerful chatter.

CHAPTER 4

NAUTICAL LESSONS

The ship's bell rang sharply and Ludlow followed Arnold to the bridge and into the wheelhouse. He just had to see what his friend was going to do.

There it was, the ship's wheel. Twelve small handles were spaced evenly along the circumference of the large wooden wheel, and it was Ludlow's main interest as his first watch drew closer.

Arnold confidently took over from the other seaman and held the wheel so that the ship continued smoothly along its course.

"Fifty-five!" The call came from the officer navigating their course.

Ludlow looked over Arnold's shoulder. The needle was pointing to fifty-four. A slight turn of the wheel by Arnold and the needle swung smoothly to fifty-five degrees.

"Looks easy," he said just loudly enough for his friend to hear.

"Hey!"

Ludlow turned to face the officer behind him. "What are you doing here?" he demanded. "Go below where you belong!"

Ludlow shouted, "Yes, sir!" and left.

Four hours. That was how long he had to wait before his watch began. Four hours until he would do something he had never done in his life—steer a ship.

Ludlow climbed into the top bunk in the sleeping quarters below the deck and rested his head on his hands. The slight swaying of the huge cargo ship didn't bother him. The initial excitement of actually being hired as a seaman was dying away and was being replaced by a brand new worry. He had lied to Captain Bhrull and told him he had experience. Oh, yes, he had lots of practice steering, knew all about it.

"Here is my letter of recommendation from Captain Kirkland." Ludlow had unfolded his precious letter and presented it at his interview. His heart had raced as the captain checked the official letterhead and read the recommendation. He had studied the nineteen-year-old youth in front of him, checked his passport, and then reaching out to shake hands said, "Welcome aboard, Walker."

It had really been as simple as that. Ludlow had been thrilled to learn that both he and Jackson had been hired. He was even more thrilled when he found out that his friend Arnold was on board the ship as well.

Stowing his gear bag in the bunkhouse and settling in had been a great excitement that first evening on board. The ship had left harbor and he had gotten along all right just imitating Arnold and helping to coil ropes or do whatever needed to be done.

Then the assignment had come. He and Arnold had been assigned to split the watch from eight o'clock that evening until four o'clock the next morning, steering.

"How do I steer? Tell me, Arnold," Ludlow had begged the next time the two met.

"Ah, man, you had better learn fast or it will be bad for you." Grabbing a piece of paper, Arnold sketched a rough compass. "When the officer calls out a number, turn the wheel and try to get the needle directly on that number. If he calls starboard, turn just a little bit. Not too much or you will overcorrect."

"What's starboard?" Ludlow asked innocently.

Arnold's eyes widened. "Walker! Starboard is right. Port is left. You have to get that into your head right now and keep it there."

"Starboard, right." Ludlow raised his right hand slightly. Grabbing a pen, he put a small s on the back of his hand. "Port, left." He added a p to his left hand.

"The thing you want to do is try to keep that needle from straying too much. The officer will yell at you if you don't keep it steady."

"Sounds easy enough," Ludlow had said with a show of bravado.

The ringing of the second bell interrupted his thoughts. Thirty minutes had passed. Thirty minutes before he began his hour-long shift. He and Arnold would split the shift every hour. Ludlow shifted his long frame on the bed. He glanced nervously at his watch.

Starboard, right. Port, left. He checked the ink marks on his hands. They did not show up much on his dark skin. That was good, for he did not want anyone to question him. He pulled out the paper with the drawing that Arnold had given him. "Keep the needle pointed toward the number the officer calls out. Try to keep it within a few degrees either to the right or to the left," he said to himself.

Over and over Ludlow repeated the directions. He held an imaginary wheel and turned it adroitly in his mind, keeping the massive ship on course. Other seamen were getting ready for bed, and Ludlow answered questions directed to him but said no more than he had to.

Would the captain fire him? Would he be put off at the first port, or even worse, be arrested for false pretenses? Was his father going to receive news that his son was in jail?

"Hold her steady," Arnold told him seriously when Ludlow went into the steering room. Ludlow put his hands on the wheel and felt it vibrate slightly under his grip. Arnold kept his own hands on the wheel as long as he dared.

"I've got to go or the officer will yell at us," Arnold said anxiously. He lifted his hands up slightly, ready to take the wheel again if he needed to. Then he turned and left abruptly.

Ludlow strained to see the compass clearly. He kept the wheel as steady as he could.

"Fifty-five!" The number was called out clearly from behind and slightly above him where the officer was charting their course.

The needle pointed to fifty-seven. Ludlow turned slightly to the left. Oh, no, sailors didn't say left; it was called port. Now the needle showed fifty-three. Ludlow turned starboard. Now it read fifty-seven again. He felt a sweat break out on his skin. With all the concentration he could muster, he moved the wheel only a fraction to port. Would nothing make that needle stay at fifty-five?

Like something with a mind of its own, the compass dropped below fifty-five all the way down to fifty-one. Although he could not feel the huge cargo ship turning beneath his feet, he was sure the officer detected their erratic course. Ludlow was not sure, but he figured there must be a compass up there and the officer could tell how far off-course he was.

Trying to get the feel of the wheel, Ludlow kept turning from starboard to port and back again. There was no sound from the officer. Ludlow desperately wanted to look back and see what his superior was doing, but he did not dare turn around. Tension was bunching up his shoulders and he ached with the strain.

The minutes ticked away. He kept trying to maintain the ship's course right on fifty-five, but like a stubborn animal, that compass needle kept switching back and forth, settling anywhere except where he wanted it.

"How long have you been steering? Not long, no?" The officer's voice startled Ludlow. His strong French accent did not cover the puzzled tone in his voice.

"I—I am not used to a gyrocompass," Ludlow stammered, impulsively saying the first thing he could think of. "I am used to a magnetic compass." He hoped that blurting out some terms he remembered from a book would sound convincing enough.

"Ha! Gyro much more easy. Let me show you," the officer said.

Yes! How gladly he would allow someone to show him!

"Look, you not just watch needle, you watch ship wheel. Then you can see to starboard or port."

Ludlow's mind clutched desperately at any piece of information given.

"What is going on here?" A booming voice rattled the darkness.

Ludlow felt something tighten in his throat. Captain Bhrull!

"Captain, this man not know gyro. Just magnetic. I show him."

"Is that true?" the captain demanded curtly.

"Yes, sir," Ludlow responded briskly.

"Well, you must come back tomorrow and I will have Benoit give you more lessons. You need to be in shape to do your watches. You, Benoit, don't neglect your primary duties. As you have time, teach Walker." With that, he was gone.

Ludlow felt the prickles on his neck gradually subside. Following Benoit's instructions, he carefully noted how each movement of the wheel affected the sensitive needle of the compass. Slowly his tense muscles relaxed, and his steering became smoother and more confident. The compass needle finally pointed to fifty-five, and Ludlow thrilled to feel the response of the massive ship under the lightest touch of his hand.

"Ludlow! Oh, my son, welcome home. Let me look at you, boy!" Ivy stepped back from embracing her son and looked at him through tears, her face wreathed in smiles. "You are looking good. I see that you get enough to eat on that boat."

"It's not a boat. It's a ship, Mom. I work on a huge cargo ship," Ludlow laughed.

"Boat, ship, whatever. Won't your siblings be surprised! And your father!"

Ludlow looked seriously at his mother. "What did Father say when he found out I had left?"

"Oh, not much. There wasn't much he could say. But never mind, if he hears you have a good job, he will be happy for you."

Three months on board the cargo ship had changed Ludlow. From being an utterly inexperienced seaman, he had advanced quickly and taken to steering the ship with confidence and ease. In his spare time he had read voraciously about seafaring techniques and quickly memorized the names of everything on the ship. No longer did he

The tall young sailor of the seas!

have to mark his hands or even deliberate whenever nautical terms were tossed out. He had earned favor on board and was accepted by the crew.

"How long can you stay?" His mother's voice brought him back to the present.

"I have a ten-day break before we sail again. Look, I brought you a present!" Ludlow pulled out a gift-wrapped box and handed it to his mother.

"Oh, son, you shouldn't have bothered," Ivy said as she unwrapped the box of chocolates, but her beaming face betrayed her sincere pleasure. "Thank you, Ludlow."

"The seafaring vagabond is back" were John Walker's first words when he returned home from his shift. His sharp eyes scanned the tall form in front of him. "So, now you are a sailor? I see you are still upright on your own two feet."

"Yes, sir," Ludlow responded with a wry grin. "I don't drink. You have taught me well."

"Humph. I hope the lessons I taught you will help you keep your senses. I imagine the company you keep will be testing that." It was true. Ludlow knew that many of his seafaring comrades were probably already hitting the bars on the island.

"I have made a strong commitment to myself never to become drunk," Ludlow said firmly, furrowing his brows and hoping his father would sense his seriousness.

"Many a boy has said that," John Walker said curtly. "You will do well to heed your own advice."

Joy flew into his arms when she came home from classes, and Gerald shook hands warmly with him that night. As they sat around the table for dinner, Ludlow told the family about his travels. He described the ports and the cities he had visited. There was a gift for each of them, purchased with the money he had earned.

"So you like it better than your job at the parts store?" John Walker inquired as they finished the celebratory cake Ivy had baked.

"Oh, yes, Father, much better. I am no longer sitting at a desk, filling out boring forms and wondering what is going on in the world and what I am missing out on. Now I get to use my muscles and my brains and get the real satisfaction of knowing I am doing a good job. I am studying and hoping for promotions. Someday I want to be one of the first officers on board the ship," Ludlow spoke earnestly.

"Big dreams," his father responded skeptically. "From what I know, there are many seamen who get tired of the long hours and hard work and abandon ship after a year or so. Then what will you do? At least you had some security with your old job."

Ludlow sighed irritably. "Father, I can do it! I am good at my job. I am learning and making a lot of money!"

"Ludlow, have another piece of cake," his mother interrupted soothingly. "Look, it is your favorite coconut cake with butter rum icing." Ivy stood up to serve another piece to Ludlow. "Joy, make some coffee. It will be good to sip while we sit on the veranda."

Gerald excused himself and Joy went to the kitchen.

"You will want to see your old friends this evening," his mother continued eagerly. "Ludlow, I can hardly wait until Sunday. All our friends will know you are back."

"Thanks, Mom, for the good dinner. Yeah, I want to go see my friends, but I don't know about church. I don't think I need that anymore." Ivy's face sobered. Ludlow looked at her keenly and felt a pang of remorse.

"Okay, okay, I'll go. It is one of the best places I can think of where we can see and be seen by everyone. Almost like a club, I guess."

Joy set a steaming cup of coffee in front of him. "Drink up, Ludlow. I want to take you with me and show you off to my friends. Such a handsome brother I have. The girls will all be competing for your attention."

"Joy!" Ivy remonstrated. How the young folks spoke these days! So bold and forward, at least according to the old rules.

Ludlow reached out and pinched Joy's ear affectionately. John Walker rose and silently left the table.

Ten days later Ludlow returned to his ship. He was glad to return to the order and schedule he was beginning to appreciate. Yes, it had been good to be home again and eat his mother's good meals. His friends had seen him and he could see the envy in the boys' eyes. The girls as well had all seemed glad to see him. Marguerite was gone, but plenty of other admiring feminine eyes had turned in his direction.

But somehow the island had seemed smaller and more constricting than he remembered. He couldn't wait to get back on the ship and on to the next adventure.

"Arnold!" Ludlow laughed and slapped his friend on the back. "I'm ready for another voyage!" He laughed aloud with joy.

CHAPTER 5

BLACKS IN THE BACK

"Good day, sir, and welcome aboard," Ludlow spoke cordially to the river pilot coming on the ship. "I am Midshipman Walker."

The American coming aboard looked sharply at Ludlow; then he glanced at his officer's uniform. "Simpson," he responded shortly.

Ludlow escorted the pilot onto the bridge and stood ready to log the pilot's instructions. By now Ludlow had four years of experience in the Merchant Marines, first becoming an able-bodied seaman, then promoted to bosun, and finally to third officer. But when it came time to navigate up the Mobile River in Alabama, regulations still required that a river pilot come aboard to advise the captain, since navigating a river was a far different story from sailing the open seas.

Simpson called out instructions and the huge vessel began to move up the mouth of the river. The city of Mobile crowded right to the edge of the water on both banks. The deep channel of the river made it possible for huge ocean-going ships to sail upriver to a more protected dock.

After the ship docked, Ludlow would have a ten-day leave, and he was eager to explore this American city. He was becoming fascinated by this huge country and took every opportunity to learn more about what made the United States so powerful and progressive.

His four years at sea had proven to be quite successful financially. He had invested in some choice property in Kingston, betting that with time the city would expand and his lot would become part of a prestigious development.

His father finally seemed reconciled with his oldest son's choice of a career. Ludlow proved himself capable of staying away from the demon of drink and invested his money wisely. The gifts he showered on his family were simply more proof that his salary was on the increase.

Ludlow felt the deck of the ship throb with the thrust of the engines. Pilot Simpson watched with a keen eye and gave occasional instructions to the helmsman, who kept the cargo ship on course.

Turning toward Ludlow, he abruptly commanded, "Get me a cup of coffee."

Ludlow calmly returned the pilot's gaze. Taking his boat whistle from his pocket, he blew it sharply. The young Jamaican boy who showed up in prompt response to the summons looked inquiringly at his officer.

"Edward, two cups of coffee, please," Ludlow requested. Turning to Simpson he asked, "Would you like anything with your coffee, sir?"

"Just black," Simpson replied curtly, looking from Ludlow to the valet.

"The usual for me," Ludlow said, and Edward hurried away to the galley. In a short time, Edward was back, carrying a tray with two cups of coffee balanced carefully on it.

"Here you go, sir." Ludlow handed Simpson a cup of the fragrant brew.

"Set it there," Simpson indicated with a nod of his head. Ludlow set the cup down on top of the instrument housing.

Taking his own cup from the tray, Ludlow nodded at Edward. "Thank you."

Simpson scowled and turned his attention back to his job. Ludlow continued to chart the course they were taking while he sipped at his coffee. Dark and strong with cream was how he always enjoyed it.

The coffee in Simpson's cup had still not been touched. Ludlow knew it was getting colder by the minute, and he also knew why Simpson was not drinking it.

In the 1950s, segregation was still rigidly observed by most people in the South. In Simpson's mind, it simply was not acceptable to drink coffee with someone who was black. Simpson assumed that any man with white skin was automatically superior to any man with black skin. It did not matter that Ludlow was a ship's officer, had moved amidships with the other officers, had his own mess boy, and dined daily with the captain; Simpson still considered Ludlow to be inferior merely because of the color of his skin.

The brusque manner in which Simpson treated Ludlow had been meant to be a slight from the moment the American had set foot on board. Ludlow had seen and felt the intended slur, but to him it was simply a sign of poor manners and he did not take offense.

In Jamaica, where there were people of many countries and nationalities, skin color and race were largely ignored. The people on the island placed far more emphasis on education and success. Ludlow had grown up with this mindset. He and his father had been treated with due respect from people of all nationalities.

Ludlow actually found it somewhat amusing that Simpson resolutely refused to drink coffee with him. Everyone on board would have recognized Ludlow as a superior to a mere river pilot, but that was not an issue Ludlow would push. He felt it was beneath his dignity to pursue something so trivial.

It was warm in Mobile—as warm as it ever got in Jamaica, but here the heat seemed to be even more intense, radiating from the streets and sidewalks. Ludlow looked around for a drinking fountain, hoping for a cooling drink.

There were two lines in front of the drinking fountains in the public square. One line was much longer than the other, and Ludlow immediately saw that the black people far outnumbered the whites. Even when there was no one in line for water at the fountain the whites used, no black person dared to use the idle fountain. They waited patiently in line, inching forward one by one.

Colored. That was what the sign said in front of the line where Ludlow stood.

"As though there are some people with no color," Ludlow said to himself. "How ignorant can people be?" He knew about racial prejudices. He had visited other cities in the American South. On board the ship he had heard stories of discrimination because of skin color, so it was not entirely new. Yet something inside him rebelled at a nation that made such distinctions based on skin color. He knew that many of the black people had deep roots in this land and, as American citizens, had equal rights with the white people.

After drinking from the fountain, Ludlow checked his little map. Someone had told him that good food was served at a restaurant several blocks away. When the city bus drew up to the curb, Ludlow bought a ticket and sat in an empty seat three rows behind the driver. They had only gone a few feet when the driver pulled to the side of the road again. Ludlow looked out the window. There was no bus stop there. He looked forward at the driver and saw him staring back in his mirror.

The bus motor idled. The driver got up and looking directly at Ludlow, he said, "The back seats are for colored folks." Ludlow looked back at the driver. Then slowly turning his head, he saw that the back seats were indeed where the black people were sitting. The few white passengers in the front seats stared indignantly at him.

Saying nothing, Ludlow simply looked out the window. He could have told the driver that he was a commissioned officer on a ship, far outranking a bus driver. He could have told this man that he was one of the first black people who had ever become an officer aboard a ship and that he did not think he needed to move to the back of anything. Ludlow straightened his shoulders and ignored the upset man as though he were a fly too insignificant to notice.

A murmur of voices from the back drew his attention to the people behind him. "C'mon, brotha, don't cause no trouble."

A businessman across the aisle said loudly, "I've got an appointment to make. I'll be late."

The tension began to build inside the bus. The driver walked back to Ludlow. "The law says black people in the back, whites up front. You're black." He said the words as though everyone should acknowledge how reasonable the segregation was.

Focusing his attention on the driver, Ludlow pulled out his passport and showed it to the man. "I am not from your country. In Jamaica, we do not discriminate."

"You sound educated," the man across the aisle said in a conciliatory tone. "Surely you understand that when you are in our country, you must abide by our rules."

Looking around inside the bus, Ludlow said pleasantly, "I don't see any rules posted telling where people of certain countries, certain skin color, or of certain education are supposed to sit, do you?" He replaced his passport in his pocket and looked silently out the window once more.

"You can't sit there," the driver said, throwing his hands up in the air. "It's not allowed."

Ludlow felt like telling him, "I *can* sit here. You say I may not, but the fact is I can. I am obviously capable of sitting here because I am sitting here." He was sure that the little lesson in proper English would be lost on the driver.

"Let's go," the businessman said loudly. "I'll be late!"

Ludlow looked at the irate bus driver. "You can drive me to the British Consul here in your city, and they will explain to you that I am a British citizen, entitled to every right that any other British citizen visiting your county has."

The driver swore in defeat, returned to his seat, jerked the bus into gear, and resumed his route.

When Ludlow reached his stop, he got up and walked toward the front of the bus. The driver waited until he was almost off and then said loudly, "The next time you *will* go to the back, you dog."

Ludlow was not one to stir up trouble. He had met with racial prejudice before and he had not intended to create a scene. Yet he felt there had been no reason for him to stoop to a ridiculous taboo being enforced by a lowly bus driver.

"Whites only." More than once he saw that sign. Others read, "Colored served around the back."

Among the blacks, Ludlow saw both an apathy that showed they were resigned to unfair treatment, and resentment among others who smoldered in indignation at conduct that was so obviously wrong.

The white people were so used to having preferential treatment that they assumed it was their unquestioned right. Ludlow had yet to meet any white person in the South who looked at the blacks as equals, although he supposed there were a few somewhere.

"He wouldn't drink his coffee. Let it get cold and there I was, enjoying my nice cup." Back on board the ship, Ludlow was telling the other officers about his experiences in Mobile.

The captain shook his head. "We see it everywhere we go in the southern United States. Places further north like New York City are not as bad for discrimination, but in the South, the whites still want to act as though they're superior."

"It will change," Ludlow said reflectively. "I have been reading some books written by activists, and I can tell that a change is coming. It's about time too." The other officers nodded.

The incidents did not disturb Ludlow greatly. He felt confident in who he was and was quite pleased that he had at twenty-three achieved goals and dreams that many older men were still struggling to reach.

Most of the time Ludlow was quite content with his life. There were times when he thought about trying to advance his career and become captain of a ship. Right now, that seemed to be the greatest achievement he could hope for.

Even his father was quite proud of him now. When he had visited his parents the last time and his father had seen his uniform, he had once more taken him on a visit to their family friends to show off his son. "Commissioned officer, Ludlow is now," he had said proudly over and over. "Has his own mess boy and eats with the other officers on board the ship."

It was good to finally have his father's approval on his life and his choice of careers. Life seemed to be smiling on the young man and Ludlow felt fulfilled and content.

CHAPTER 6

MILLICENT

Humming softly, Millicent deftly ironed her blouse. She heard the front door of her Manhattan home opening but paid little attention to who was entering until she heard male voices. She parked her iron and went out into the hall to investigate the source of the laughter and banter she could hear.

"Oh, my," she breathed softly to herself, her dark eyes widening. She was struck by the tall form and good looks of the young man standing in the hall with her cousin Vincent. She ducked quickly back into the room where she had been ironing and checked herself in the mirror.

Millicent was used to receiving admiring looks herself. Vibrant and outgoing, she was quite popular among her friends. She even had a sort-of boyfriend, but she had not committed herself to Cecil. It was convenient to have someone to escort her and take her out to dinner, but she was still keeping her options open.

"I want you to come meet my friend," Vincent said a moment later, entering the living room with the handsome stranger in tow. "You will like Ludlow."

Shaking hands with the tall newcomer, Millicent was impressed by his good manners and courtly behavior.

"I am delighted to meet you," he said, bowing slightly as they were introduced. "New York City has many beautiful sights, but I am most impressed by the beauty of the young ladies I meet." Ludlow's eyes, smiling as he looked at Millicent, convinced her that the compliment was sincere.

The evening progressed rapidly as the young people became better acquainted. When Ludlow rose to leave, he shook hands with Millicent again. "It has been a pleasure to meet you, and I have enjoyed my evening tremendously," he said softly as his dark eyes looked deeply into Millicent's. "Would you have dinner with me tomorrow evening?" he continued as they reached the front door. "I would love to get to know you better."

"Millicent, close the door. It will get cold in here!" Her mother, Barbara Dennings, spoke sharply. "Who are you talking to anyway?"

Stepping outside the house and closing the door, Millicent looked up at Ludlow. "I would enjoy that," she said sincerely. "What time may I expect you?"

"My first paycheck seemed enormous to me," Ludlow recounted, leaning across the restaurant table and smiling at the memory. "That was four years ago, and I still consider myself fortunate when I think how my finances have improved."

Millicent savored another bite of her succulent steak. "I know that feeling as well, because after I graduated from college, I was hired almost immediately as a secretary in the Federal Government Housing Division."

Ludlow took his knife and neatly cut a portion from his steak. "How long have you worked there?" he inquired.

"It will be three years in May," Millicent replied. Turning her attention to the food, she said, "This is a delicious meal." Looking around at the other diners she added, "And an excellent restaurant."

Ludlow smiled. He was pleased by his choice and he could tell that Millicent was impressed too.

"Are you seeing anyone else?" Ludlow asked suddenly.

"What do you mean, 'anyone else'?" Millicent teased. "Am I seeing you?"

"I hope so," Ludlow said. "I would like to think we will be seeing a lot of each other in the two months I have here in New York City."

"Oh, well, there is Cecil," Millicent laughed. "I see him from time to time."

Ludlow felt a twinge of fear touch his spine. "Cecil?" he asked sharply.

"Just another young man from Jamaica," Millicent said with a sparkle. "Like you."

"Do you want to take a walk?" Ludlow had suddenly lost his appetite for food. "The evening is not too chilly, is it? Perhaps you know of a nice place to walk."

"There is a park not far from here," Millicent told him. "Yes, I would enjoy a nice walk after such a lovely dinner."

Three days later when Ludlow knocked at the door of the Dennings' house, Millicent opened the door. "Ludlow, come in!" Her voice was warm and welcoming. "Come in and meet my friend."

A young man stood as they entered the living room. Ludlow noted scornfully that he was hardly any taller than Millicent.

"Cecil, this is Ludlow," Millicent said with a twinkle in her eye. "He is also from Jamaica. Ludlow, meet Cecil."

Ludlow tried to size up Millicent's friend. He could see he definitely held the advantage over Cecil in height, for his own six feet two inches dwarfed the shorter man. Secretly, Ludlow thought he probably surpassed Cecil in looks as well. He hoped Millicent felt that way.

"No, I have never lived in Kingston," Cecil said in answer to Ludlow's first question. "I visited there several times, but I have lived in New York City for the past five years." He looked at Millicent and smiled. Something about the way he looked at her seemed almost possessive, and Ludlow found himself stiffening.

Millicent laughed as she looked at the two rivals. Turning to Ludlow, she said brightly, "You know, I thought you two might have some things in common. But I guess it's like the people who assume that because I live in New York City, I must know what every New Yorker's life is like. I suppose it's the same in Jamaica."

Ludlow tried to smile at her, but he had to force his lips into an awkward curve. He glanced at Cecil with poorly concealed disdain.

"Well, it took me quite a while to learn the culture when I first came to

America," Cecil said, glancing first at Ludlow and then at Millicent with a laugh. "Remember the first time we met at Sal's party? I told you then that the food was so different." He leaned back in his chair and laughed loudly.

Ludlow failed to see the humor in this remark. "I don't find the culture here that much different from our culture in Kingston. Our home was quite similar to yours, Millicent, except we had more space outside."

"Well, we didn't live in mud huts either," Cecil snapped. Turning to Millicent he said, "You know, I just dropped in. I will stop by later. Perhaps you will be free then."

Millicent saw him politely to the door and then returned to the living room.

"Did I tell you that I invested in property in Kingston?" Ludlow asked her. "I bought this really nice lot in an area where developers are investing for housing. It's just outside the city and overlooks the Caribbean." Frowning suddenly, he asked almost peevishly, "Does Cecil have a steady job?"

Millicent stifled a grin. It was rather fun having two young men competing for her attention! "Yes, he works for a construction firm," she told the serious young man.

A knock on the door interrupted their conversation. It was Cecil.

"I forgot my gloves," he said, looking from Millicent to Ludlow. "I left them here somewhere." Millicent located the gloves for him and Cecil went out the door, scowling but keeping his eyes from Ludlow.

"I'm surprised he doesn't have more than one pair of gloves," Ludlow said stiffly. "He must not have much money."

"Let's not talk about Cecil," Millicent laughed. "How about going for a walk instead?"

The opportunity to have Millicent all to himself pleased Ludlow. He determined to push Cecil out of his mind and, hopefully, out of Millicent's life as well.

"You will write, won't you?" Ludlow's voice was soft. "Here are the dates and addresses where you can send the letters." He slid a piece of paper across the table.

"I will miss you," Millicent murmured with a sigh.

"The evenings spent with you have been the best times of my life," Ludlow said with feeling. "Please tell me you will not forget me and that you will write to me."

"I don't think I could ever forget you," Millicent said gently. "I have enjoyed these evenings too much to pass them off lightly."

Ludlow felt his heart beat rapidly. Those were the words he was longing to hear.

"I will come to see you every chance I get," Ludlow assured her. "Even when we dock in Philadelphia, I can get here by train in several hours."

Dining for the last time at their favorite restaurant was a bittersweet experience for the two young friends. The next day Ludlow had to leave with his ship.

"Maybe I could get a job with a different ship that would sail to New York City more frequently," Ludlow said eagerly. "Then we could spend more time together."

"Would switching ships be difficult?"

"Well, I might have to take a lower position, but I think it would be worth it if I could see you more often, my dear."

Millicent traced an aimless pattern on the tablecloth with her fork. "I would appreciate that," she said finally.

"You will wait for me, won't you?" Ludlow asked. For a moment, he thought about Cecil. Would she start seeing that guy again if Ludlow was no longer around?

As if reading his mind, Millicent said, "I really don't want to go out with anyone except you."

Ludlow felt like shouting, but he managed to restrain his voice in the busy restaurant. "Oh, Millicent, I will miss you terribly."

Dear Millicent,

Ludlow stared at the blank white paper on the table in front of him. Trees shaded the place where he sat, and he gazed thoughtfully across the

harbor where his ship was berthed. The charms of the port city in Venezuela had utterly failed to capture him during this brief layover while
they waited to unload their cargo and take aboard another load. Ludlow
had other things on his mind.

*When I think how destiny brought us together through your cousin, I
know we were meant to be together. For some reason, I think you share
that sentiment.*

*I remember the first time I met you, coming down the hall toward me.
Actually, that was not quite the first time, because I saw a picture of you
inside your front hall. My first thought was,* What a beautiful girl!

*Then, when I saw you in person, you were even more beautiful to me! I
remember how your brown eyes sparkled when you talked, and your ready
smile was the sunshine that could warm any place if we were only together.*

Ludlow laid down his pen and reread the words he had written. He
pursed his lips and rubbed his thigh. How could mere words convey the
deep feelings of his heart?

A vendor approached with a pushcart of soft drinks, tinkling his little
bell. Ludlow pulled out his wallet and bought a cold bottle of Pepsi. His
mouth was unusually dry just then.

Carefully wiping his hands, Ludlow picked up his pen once more.

*I recall with fondness the times we spent together, exploring your great
city. I remember eating together at our favorite restaurants, the soft lights
shining on your hair and catching the highlights. Your laughter was music
to my soul, and I can still hear the echoes in my mind.*

*Remember the time we got caught in a rain shower when we were down
by the Hudson River and we had to run for shelter under a bridge? Running
with you and splashing through the puddles like little children is a memory
I will keep forever.*

*All these incidents make my heart race whenever I think of you, and they
give me reason to believe we should be together for the rest of our lives.*

Lifting his eyes to the branches above him, Ludlow did not even see the pattern of the leaves against the blue sky. Rather, he seemed to see Millicent's face gazing back at him. He pulled her picture from his wallet and stared at the smiling face in the photo.

Just putting down the words, "be together for the rest of our lives" on his paper had sent a surge of pure joy through his entire body. He could barely write.

Millicent, my dear, I am asking you to marry me.

There, he had written the words right out. He reread his sentence.

I want to spend the rest of my life with you and live with the one I love forever.

Ludlow no longer cared if it was redundant.

I want to live with you all of my days. Forever and forever, side by side, our hearts bound together in love.

His pen raced across the paper, capturing the overflowing sentiments of his heart.

I know this is not news to you, for surely you felt our love for each other growing as we spent time together. Now, I ask you to be my wife.

As soon as I arrive in New Jersey, I will take the train and come to see you. With great joy I anticipate your answer and the chance to personally ask you to be my wife and hear your acceptance to my proposal.

With all my love,
Ludlow Walker

Folding the letter carefully, Ludlow put it in an envelope, addressed it by memory, and got up. He looked around for a post office box. For a moment he paused before dropping his letter into the slot. Then he pushed it in, drew a big breath, and imagined Millicent opening it about a week later and spreading it out in front of her. His heart raced at the thought.

It would be more than three weeks before his ship would reach the New Jersey shores. It was a long time to wait for an answer from the girl he loved.

―――――――――――――――

As his ship sailed north, Ludlow swabbed the decks, cleaned the kitchen, and kept himself busy with menial tasks.

"Yes, sir," he replied briskly to the captain whenever he was asked to do some lowly task. He clearly understood the expectations of the officers on board the ship.

At first it had been a trying task to voluntarily demote himself from being a ship's officer and take a job with another shipping firm to get work that would bring him close to New York City almost monthly. Going from the preferential treatment that his rank had offered him as third officer to doing the most menial tasks was only acceptable because that meant he could see Millicent more frequently.

"How love changes things," Arnold had said when Ludlow told his friend of his plans. "This must be the real thing." He had looked keenly at his friend. "You know, we two made history by being the first black Jamaicans to reach our rank on board a ship. Will you actually take a lower position again?"

"If it makes it possible to see Millicent, I will gladly do it," Ludlow had told him without hesitation.

Now, pausing for a moment as the ship slowly followed the path his heart had already taken, Ludlow said to himself, "Oh, Millicent, I am coming! I am coming to pledge myself to you!"

He stared out over the vast expanse of ocean all around them. "I am coming!" he suddenly yelled impulsively and then quickly looked around to see if any of the ship hands had heard him. Facing north he yelled once more, "Millicent, I am coming!"

7

THE BIG APPLE

The spacious interior of Saint Philip's Cathedral swelled with organ music, and the hundreds of people waiting quietly in the pews sat in anticipation as the familiar strains heightened their expectancy.

Outside, the December winds whipped snow along the streets and the cold pushed people inside quickly. December 10, 1961. The wedding day had finally arrived, carefully planned to coincide with Ludlow's shore leave. From the moment Millicent had given him the answer to his proposal, Ludlow had longed for this day.

Now, dressed in a white shirt and tuxedo, he stood tall and straight on the raised platform in the front, his eyes fixed steadily on the closed double doors at the back of the auditorium. He took a slow, deep breath and scanned the crowd briefly.

Most of the faces looking up at him were those of recent acquaintances. His immediate family from Jamaica was not there, although a few cousins were in attendance. Ludlow swallowed and wet his lips. He wished his mother could see him now. He wished Gerald and Joy could have come. Or his father.

From the time he had arrived at Millicent's home three months earlier and she had said yes, the wedding plans had gone ahead with dizzying speed. "Everything," Millicent's mother had said, "I want everything for my daughter's wedding." Barbara Dennings had gotten her way. From the catered buffet reception to the hired limousine that waited outside, no expense had been spared.

"Let's just go away and get married," Ludlow had suggested to Millicent at one point. "Do we need all this preparation?"

"Oh, every girl needs her wedding," Millicent had laughed, slipping her arm through his. "Besides, Mama would have a fit if we did that."

Ludlow had smiled at his fiancé. "Yes, you are right."

Now the day was here. A tremor of something Ludlow could not quite identify ran up his spine. The organ music swelled into a crescendo and the rear doors opened. The crowd all rose to their feet and turned to face the wedding party.

Swathed in white, Millicent entered. Her eyes immediately found Ludlow's, and the radiant smile that was directed at him made Ludlow's heart beat rapidly. He beamed back at her and watched as she came slowly up the aisle.

Standing in front of their guests, the two repeated their wedding vows after the vicar.

"I present to you Mr. and Mrs. Ludlow Walker." The words rang out in the hushed church. Then, as the vicar nodded at them, Ludlow bent over and kissed his bride. The crowd erupted into clapping and cheering, the music began again, and the beaming couple swept down the aisle.

"Hello, Mrs. Millicent Walker," Ludlow said with a grin from the back seat of the roomy limo. He slipped his arm tenderly around his new bride.

Millicent giggled, "I will have to get used to that; it doesn't sound like me!"

Pulling her close, Ludlow gently drew her head onto his shoulder. "It is you, Mrs. Walker! My wife, my love."

"Careful of my dress!" Millicent cautioned, spreading her voluminous skirts in front of her. "I must stay pretty for the reception!"

"You are not only pretty, you are beautiful," Ludlow replied with a laugh. "Oh, Millicent, the day we have planned for so long is here! We are actually married!" As they were chauffeured through the streets of Manhattan, the happy couple was in a world of their own.

The music, flowers, candles, and laden tables set a festive mood. The guests at the reception all wished the young couple success and a wonderful life together. As Ludlow escorted his bride around the room, many of the guests congratulated Millicent on her handsome and well-mannered groom.

Once more, Ludlow wished his family could see him. He wanted Millicent to meet his mother, and he would have loved to show off his beautiful bride to his father.

He thought briefly about his boyhood on the island and his early dreams about leaving the island and getting a position on board a ship. Now here he was, in America, with a beautiful bride by his side and with love deep in his heart. The present surely smiled on them and Ludlow felt confident that their future together would be even brighter.

The happy couple left the reception amid the usual cheers and good wishes from their guests and then, finally, the two of them were alone. Millicent, no longer careful about her dress, pressed close to Ludlow's side and sighed gently. She looked up into Ludlow's face and ran her fingers over his chin. Ludlow took her slim hand in his and drew it up to his face. They were married!

Ludlow ran down the steps toward the dock and watched in dismay as the huge cargo ship slowly pulled away. He turned and scanned the port. There! The pilot boat was still at the dock. Ludlow raced toward the boat, his long legs eating up the short distance.

"Sir, that is my ship! I was delayed by the train and I need to report to work!" Ludlow called respectfully to the helmsman of the boat, his breath coming in short gasps.

"Let me see your identification papers."

Ludlow drew out his ID card and presented it.

"Get on," the helmsman said with a nod. "Lucky for you we hadn't left yet."

As they pulled away from the New Jersey shore, Ludlow paid no attention to the shoreline behind him. He watched as his ship moved out into the harbor and waited for the pilot boat. Maneuvering the enormous ships in a crowded harbor was difficult, so channel pilots safely guided the giant cargo ships out to open water and then returned to shore with the pilot boat. As the pilot boat came alongside the ship, Ludlow scrambled up the Jacob's ladder fastened to the side and boarded the ship.

"Reporting for work, sir," Ludlow said respectfully, facing the captain and standing at attention.

"Shore leave was over two hours ago," the captain replied, frowning at the young man.

"Yes, sir." Ludlow knew he could try to explain why he was late, but as a former officer, he also knew the rules. No seaman was ever to be late and there really were no excuses.

"I imagine it had something to do with public transportation," the captain guessed correctly, "but you know there are no excuses."

He should have left home earlier. He wanted to tell the captain how difficult it was to leave the little apartment that was their home now and tear himself away from Millicent, knowing they might not see each other for a month while his ship sailed down to South America and back again.

"Three days docked pay," the captain finally declared.

"Yes, sir."

Ouch. They needed all the money they could make. Millicent's job paid well, but Ludlow had assured her from the beginning that he would not allow her wages to be used for their living expenses. He was still making payments on his real estate investments in Jamaica. Furthermore, after he had taken a job as an able-bodied seaman instead of his former officer's position, he had also taken a cut in pay.

"No shore leave in Venezuela," the captain continued. "Now, report to the bosun."

"Yes, sir." Ludlow turned and left.

No shore leave. Staying on board the vessel while in dock could be rather boring, but Ludlow was used to life on board the huge cargo ships. He could spend the time writing letters to Millicent and send the missives with one of his more fortunate comrades to mail on shore. Besides, this would be his last voyage, so it really didn't matter much.

After almost seven years at sea, this was all to end now.

"I didn't marry you to see you for only several days every other month or so," Millicent had said at his last shore leave, her tear-stained face pressed against his chest. "That isn't marriage to me."

"I know, my dear," Ludlow had replied, his own heart hurting deeply as he thought of the coming separation. "But I don't know what else to do! I really only know a sailor's life."

Millicent had sobbed quietly as her arms tightened around her husband. "You could get a job here in New York City. You are smart and a good worker. Surely something is available."

Ludlow said nothing at the time. He wasn't sure that he could find another job. First of all, he would have to apply for an American working visa. His passport was Jamaican.

"I'll do it," he had finally told Millicent. "When I get back from this voyage, I will leave and look for work here. Here with you!"

They had laughed and clung close to each other. "Oh, that will be wonderful!" Millicent had murmured through her tears.

Ludlow once more felt the fingers of apprehension creep up his spine as he looked into his future. Would he be able to get a job?

"Put your completed application there." The lady behind the desk barely glanced at Ludlow as he handed her the completed form.

"Ma'am, will you let me know the outcome? I really need this job."

A pair of indifferent eyes looked at him from behind a pair of glasses. "If you are accepted for an interview, we will let you know."

"But I won't be notified if my application is not accepted?" Ludlow tried to speak calmly, but his voice rose slightly as he leaned forward.

Looking up and down at the tall figure in front of her, the woman said with a shake of her head, "No."

A door opened behind the lady's desk and a middle-aged gentleman walked out, headed for the stairwell.

"Then, ma'am, I will be back in several days to see if my application has been submitted and find out if there will be an interview scheduled." Ludlow's voice was modulated and polite, yet serious.

"No need," the woman said, shaking her head again and turning to the paper work on her desk. "We will let you know."

Ludlow felt his hopes plunging. It was the usual scenario. The airlines all wanted workers with experience and Ludlow wondered again how anyone was to get experience if no one hired anyone inexperienced. He longed to show the employers that he could learn anything.

Ludlow's search for a job had been long and fruitless. At first he had thought it ludicrous that a ship's officer would have to lower himself to apply for menial jobs, but as the days wore on and there had been no openings, he laid his pride aside and tried for any job.

"I will try the airline companies first," he had told Millicent. "I think if you learn the procedures well, there is room for advancement just like on board a ship."

So here he was, in the office of KLM airlines, applying for any position they would give him.

"Are you from Jamaica?" The sound of a man's voice caught Ludlow by surprise as he was turning away from the desk in disappointment.

"Yes, sir, I am," he replied listlessly.

The speaker was the man who had come out of an office behind the receptionist.

"I thought so. The accent, you know." The man smiled and walked across the room toward Ludlow. "Steven Prantis," he said, extending a hand. "Glad to meet you. I was born and raised in Kingston." Ludlow took the proffered hand and introduced himself. "I didn't know my Jamaican accent was so pronounced," he laughed.

"Not hard to pick out when that is what you have spoken all your life," Mr. Prantis smiled.

Then he looked more closely at Ludlow. "You are applying for a job?"

The smile faded from Ludlow's face and he looked at his shoes for a moment. Then looking at Mr. Prantis' face again he said, "Yes, sir."

"I have a job opening in the kitchen," Mr. Prantis said bluntly, looking keenly at Ludlow. "Washing dishes."

Ludlow bowed slightly. "I would welcome any job," he said sincerely.

"Any experience?" The dreaded question sent Ludlow's hopes plunging.

Wetting his lips, Ludlow said honestly, "No, sir. But I would be willing to learn."

Mr. Prantis looked at the earnest young man in front of him. "You would be willing to work long, hard hours sweating in a kitchen? You appear to be a man of education and perhaps even a businessman."

Ludlow wanted to explain his situation, but he did not think it would help his possibilities any, so he merely said, "I would be willing to work hard and learn."

Turning toward the desk where the receptionist was busy with her duties, Mr. Prantis said, "Mabel, please let me see this young man's application." Then turning to Ludlow, he requested, "Step right this way."

"Here they come," Ludlow called out to Tontu as he pulled the luggage from the undercarriage compartment of the huge airliner. Grabbing the suitcases and other luggage quickly from their places, Ludlow tossed them on the conveyer belt leading from the plane down to where Tontu placed them on the luggage truck.

Wearing ear mufflers was a necessity. Even with his ears covered, Ludlow could hear the familiar roar of the jet engines as flights arrived and departed from Idlewild Airport all day. The airport traffic, even in 1965, was heavy and increasing each year.

Ludlow felt the stinging smart of his sleep-deprived eyes as he grabbed suitcase after suitcase. He knew he had to finish his shift before he could sink into bed for several hours of sleep.

As with many menial jobs, washing dishes had allowed Ludlow to get a foot in the door at KLM, and he continued watching for other available positions with the company. After six months of hot, sweaty work loading and unloading dishes from huge dishwashers, Ludlow had found an opening as a baggage handler and gratefully left the kitchen. Now, almost three years later, Ludlow was working two jobs—one shift for KLM and another shift for Pan American.

"Sometimes I wonder if we have any more time together than we did when you were a seaman," Millicent told Ludlow before he fell asleep on the couch. "You are gone sixteen hours every day and I am gone eight. When our schedules happen to align properly, we see each other."

"I know," Ludlow said sleepily. "I know. But at least we have this house now. And with a baby coming, we can finally afford to have you quit work."

"At least then I will be able to see you every time you get off work, and you will get to see our baby."

Ludlow did not answer. He had fallen asleep.

Millicent sighed and pulled a blanket over him. He would probably not wake up until it was time for him to get up at midnight and begin his first shift with KLM. Then at nine he would begin his second shift at Pan Am and come home at five, exhausted.

At least their finances had improved since their marriage. Moving from Brooklyn to Queens and buying a house had been a smart move. The renters on the other side of their duplex paid the mortgage, and Ludlow's investments in Wall Street were rising in value.

Yes, they had worked hard. Money was not an issue, for Ludlow worked diligently and saved his earnings. He even formed an investment group and taught others how to pick winning stocks and was paid dividends from them.

Millicent sighed as she went to her lonely bed. Although life had smiled on them and they were eager to begin their family now that finances were secure, there were times when she wondered if all the hard work was worth the time they sacrificed away from each other. Maybe having a baby would help. Maybe having a child in their home would bring them closer together again. She glanced pensively at Ludlow, snoring softly on the sofa, and sighed wistfully.

CHAPTER 8

TROPICAL PARK

"The entire hundred-acre area is for sale." Emory King waved a hand out over the Belizean landscape. The tropical heat was tempered by the coastal wind, blowing steadily from the sea only a few miles away. Ludlow wiped his brow and looked over the extensive tract of land.

"This is a lot like Jamaica," he observed once more. "I feel at home here."

"Think, Walker, how rich you would have become if you could have made the right investments thirty years ago in Jamaica. Belize now offers you that same potential. This country is poised for rapid development. Foreigners are moving in because of the low prices and stable government. In seven or ten years, this land will be worth . . . who knows how much?"

Ludlow deliberated. His keen mind was already imagining his investments doubled or even tripled. Truly this was a land of opportunity.

"Have your attorney draw up the papers." Ludlow spoke decisively and Mr. King reached out to shake hands on the deal.

"Now I want you to see Tropical Park," Mr. King said, turning toward his car. "This is the real money maker."

The two friends headed west from Belize City, and Mr. King turned onto a wide graveled road. "Most of these lots are already sold," Emory said as he slowed the car. "They've been sold to foreign investors as well as Belizeans. This is already the coveted neighborhood for residents who want to build their new homes in a private, secluded area."

Amid the coastal pines Ludlow saw large tile-roofed houses separated by generous green lawns. "How big are the lots?" he inquired.

"These first ones are only several acres each, but up there," Emory said as he pointed to the top of a small knoll, "we have five-acre lots. And," he paused dramatically, "I still have ten-acre lots for sale at the end. For the really big estates."

Ludlow felt his excitement rising. This was the life! These big business deals were the kind he had long been dreaming of.

"Listen, Ludlow, I like your entrepreneurial spirit. I want to make a deal with you. You go back to New York City and market my lots. I'll let you have the small lots for $600 and whatever you can sell them for will be your profit. The big ones you can have for $6,000; I know you can sell them for $10,000," Emory said seriously. "I have over fifty lots. You do the math. This will be big money for you."

Ludlow felt a wave of pure adrenaline. This *was* big money. "What makes you offer this deal to me?" He turned to face the businessman.

"One reason is because you have vision. And you are not afraid of taking risks. When you said you would take the entire 103 acres, I saw that you knew where the riches are. Plus, I have studied you the last several days and can tell you are not lazy. You have ambition."

It was true. Ludlow was proud to have Emory King recognize his abilities.

"How did you come into your money?" Emory wanted to know. Then interrupting himself he said, "Now look here. Can't you see this entire back area built up with large mansions and estates? Perfect weather, low labor costs, and a plentiful supply of building materials. How could anyone go wrong?"

Ludlow nodded and then addressed the previous question. "I worked for both KLM and Pan American airlines for about eight years and was advanced into managerial positions with both airlines. I also invested in Wall Street, and I have property in Jamaica that has doubled in value." With a shrug and a laugh, Ludlow continued, "I guess hard work and lots of luck."

The hot sun shone brilliantly on the tropical paradise as the two continued their talk of the wealth that would surely be coming their way.

"Ludlow! Will you get the door?" Millicent called from the bedroom where she was getting Dawn into her pajamas for the night. She heard her husband come out of the living room and walk into the front hall.

"Come in, Mr. Zablonski. Hello, Mr. Thwaite, and Dr. Thompson. You're right on time."

The men entered their hall and before Ludlow could escort them into the den in their basement, the doorbell rang again.

"Mrs. Walker," the men bowed slightly as Millicent carried her daughter into the hall. Millicent nodded and smiled in return. More men were coming into the house and eventually Ludlow escorted them all into the den.

"Now gentlemen," Ludlow began when they were all comfortable, "you have come to hear more about Tropical Park. You have read the brochures and listened to the testimonials." Ludlow moved easily into his introduction.

For more than an hour, he told his audience about Belize, speaking knowledgeably about the land of palms, sunshine, and fair weather. He answered their questions about building codes, availability of skilled laborers, and matters of foreign investment.

"Mrs. Walker, your husband is a wonderful salesman," Dr. Thompson said after Millicent had put her daughter to bed and had gone downstairs to serve drinks to the men.

"Yes, he is," Millicent laughed as she glanced over to where Ludlow was pushing a form across his desk for a client to sign.

"I will be buying two lots," the doctor told her in a low voice. "I am most impressed by the plans I see on the charts and by the statistics your husband shared."

"You surely are making a wise decision," Millicent assured the doctor with a smile.

She could see that Ludlow was in his element as the wealthy and the would-be wealthy eagerly bought up the lots her husband recommended.

"You have a beautiful home here," the doctor continued. "For a young couple, you have done quite well financially, I would think."

It was true. Ludlow's investments were paying off handsomely, his two jobs paid all their living expenses, and the other side of their duplex was still making the payments on the house. Yes, life was going very well for the Walkers.

"I am going to build a motel on some land in Tropical Park," Ludlow announced to Millicent one evening at dinner. "I want a five-star motel."

"Daddy! You can't have stars for motels," Dawn laughed, her bright eyes sparkling. At four, she was quick to pick up on any conversation.

"We will have stars," Ludlow laughed with his daughter. "Five stars mean it will be a very, very nice motel."

"Oh, good! I want to sleep there!" Dawn clapped her hands.

"You know, Millicent, I want to move to Belize when the motel is built. I want to live there." Ludlow watched his wife closely for her reaction.

"Oh, Ludlow, leave New York?" Then with a shrug she said, "I have lived here all my life. I would hardly know what to do anywhere else."

"You will be the queen of the motel," Ludlow said, flashing a grin at her. "There will be pineapples, bananas, mangos, and all manner of citrus fruit for you. Sunshine, warm weather, and a swimming pool you can swim in every day. No more cold, slush, and ice every winter."

"I think I am being given the salesman speech," Millicent said with a wry grin.

"Now in Tropical Park you will no longer have to deal with ice and snow, for it is warm all year round," Dawn piped up, mimicking her father.

"Someone is going to make a wonderful salesperson," said Ludlow, laughing and looking at Millicent.

"Well, she has been hearing that speech for over a year," Millicent said, beaming at their daughter. "Dawn has a wonderful memory for a little girl."

"If I liquidate all our holdings here, we will have working capital to build our motel," Ludlow continued. "We will start by building the first phase, which will include living quarters for us and a restaurant and bar."

Millicent felt a niggling uneasiness as she listened to Ludlow's enthusiastic plans. Did she want to move away from her family and relatives? Move to a foreign country?

"Emory King has told me he will be one of my first guests, and he assured me that when word gets out, our motel will be frequented by the important government officials in Belize," Ludlow continued. "I see opportunity in this venture."

"Dawn, you bring that sweater back." Millicent straightened her weary back and called to her little girl scampering down the stairs. "I need to pack it for you."

"I want to wear my sweater right now!" Dawn turned to face her mother, her lower lip sticking out in that determined look Millicent knew all too well.

"Sweetie, this is a warm day. You'll get much too hot with a sweater. Besides, we need to pack it because you will need it sometime in Belize," Millicent remonstrated wearily. "At least I suppose you'll need a sweater sometime, although it sounds as though it never cools off down there," Millicent murmured to herself and sighed. Whatever were they getting themselves into?

She surveyed the clothes she had packed for her daughter. It was hard to decide what to take along and what to leave behind. Would they be able to buy the clothes they needed? How much could they leave behind and still have a decent life in Belize? Ludlow made the country sound like paradise, but she was sure it had a lot of drawbacks.

It was really no use asking Ludlow. His distracted answer was always the same. "Everything will be all right. Oh, yes, you can buy anything you need down there. No, honey, our life will not change that drastically."

Returning to the present, Millicent sighed again and called sternly to Dawn, "You bring that sweater up here right now if you want to take it along to Belize. I am sure you don't want me to leave it out of your box."

"Belize, Belize," Dawn sang, suddenly becoming compliant as the novelty of their move registered in her mind. "Will there be crocodiles there?" she asked, her large eyes growing wide at the thought.

"I only hope crocodiles will be the biggest worry we have," Millicent grumbled, not even caring that she was complaining. Unwillingly, she remembered Ludlow's persuasive words.

"Millicent," Ludlow had said in his suave and charming way, "our life in Belize will be so easy. The motel will bring in a great income and we can hire maids and cooks to do all your work. You won't need to lift a finger. If you want to come back to New York to visit, it will be easy to do. Look how many lots have already been sold. The motel is being built and our unit will soon be finished." Ludlow had waved his papers about as he spoke enthusiastically. "Then someday soon we will build our big house, and it will be nicer than anything we have ever lived in."

"It is probably true," Millicent admitted to herself. "Ludlow has always had big dreams and those dreams have eventually turned into reality." She looked fondly around the nice home they had enjoyed for the past few years. "That is just the problem with me," she said in a low tone. "It is too nice and I enjoy living here with my friends and relatives."

There. She had voiced the real obstacle in her mind. Not only was she leaving this house, she was leaving her family. She was sure she would miss her mother acutely.

"Belize, Belize," Dawn continued her song, waltzing around in her room. "Belize, Belize, here we come."

Millicent closed the lid of the trunk and stood up. Surveying the room, she pressed her lips together, her mind spinning in an endless cycle of questions and apprehensions about the impending move. She wished she could be as excited as Dawn and Ludlow were about moving.

CHAPTER 9

MOPAN

The car stopped in the motel yard and the driver hopped out, opened the back door, and helped the lady guest out.

Mrs. Susan Jensen took a deep breath and inhaled deeply. "Sunshine! Goodbye, snow and mud and cold and slush in Minnesota! Hello, sunshine and warmth and blue skies and relaxation in paradise!"

The man in the back seat had gotten out and now joined his wife. "We get to enjoy this for two whole weeks!" he exclaimed. "Wow, what a beautiful place!" He looked at the tidy units of the motel and with a sweeping glance found the patio outside the restaurant and bar, with the tables under umbrellas to shade the diners from the bright sunlight.

"And a pool, just like the brochure said, Herman." Susan pointed toward the sparkling blue water and turned to her husband. "I will always be grateful to you for choosing this wonderful place in Belize for our vacation."

The door to the reception room was open, and the couple turned as Ludlow came to meet them. "Mr. and Mrs. Jensen?" he greeted them pleasantly. "I am Ludlow Walker and I welcome you to Mopan. We hope you will find everything you need and a few pleasant surprises you did not anticipate."

"Mr. Walker, you are the owner of this fabulous place, are you not? This is an absolute paradise." Susan gazed at her host. "Why did you name it Mopan? Is it some ancient Indian name or something? It sounds so . . .

so exotic, or Belizean, or something. I am sure there is some intriguing history about this place. I can just feel it."

"You are right, ma'am," Ludlow replied smoothly. "Mopan is the name of the river that flows through the property and it is an old Belizean name. We will have to do more research about the local history. Perhaps you could do some study about it and let us know."

Susan laughed delightedly. "I would love that. Oh, Herman, isn't this a delightful place?"

Fred Lee, the hotel manager, came outside to join the group. "This is Fred from Canada. He will take good care of you, and if you need anything, just see him," Ludlow finished, introducing the middle-aged man to the Jensens.

Then turning to Susan, Ludlow invited, "Ma'am, will you come with me and get something to drink while your husband registers?"

"You are so kind," Susan laughed and then turned to her husband. "Herman, come and join us when you have registered. Oh, I can't wait to look inside one of these tropical units."

"Come right this way." Ludlow took her elbow and steered her toward the motel rooms. "You can see your rooms first and then we will go get that drink."

The bellhop had already removed the guests' luggage from the car trunk and was carrying it up the path to their room.

"Look, there's an air conditioner!" Susan cried. Turning to Ludlow, she continued confidentially, "I was reluctant to come to Belize at first because I don't like it when it gets too hot, but when I read that you had all the modern amenities, I gained confidence this wouldn't be some primitive place where I would be uncomfortable."

"We pride ourselves in providing five-star accommodations," Ludlow boasted confidently. "Our guests come from all over the world and quite a few people are investing in Tropical Park, planning to retire here in this wonderful country."

Susan smiled mischievously and laid her hand on Ludlow's arm. "Don't tell Herman, but I secretly decided that if we liked it well enough, I would ask you about investment property." Taking in the neat room, the small refrigerator under the efficiency sink, and the tropical décor, she smiled and nodded.

"Okay, let's go get that drink. The flight down here was not so bad, but I need something cold to complement this tropical feel."

As the two moved across the courtyard, Millicent emerged from their living quarters with an armload of towels.

"Mrs. Jensen, meet my wife Millicent."

Susan smiled and said with delight, "You mean you live right here in this wonderful paradise? Oh, I envy you two."

"There are actually three of us," Millicent smiled as Dawn came out of their open doorway.

"This is your daughter? How beautiful you are. What is your name?"

Dawn smiled up at the guest. "My name is Dawn and I am seven years old."

Another car drove onto the compound and three men got out and headed for the restaurant.

"Come, dear," Millicent said, taking Dawn's hand. "I need to take these to Unit 21." Turning to her husband, she said in a low voice, "Once again, Teresa did not show up."

Ludlow muttered a hasty "Oh" before taking Susan once more by the elbow and escorting her to the patio where he left her in the care of a waiter.

When Millicent returned, having left Dawn outside, Ludlow was drumming his fingers on the tabletop. "Millicent, it did not look good to have you taking towels to the units. I mean, we are a first-class hotel and to see you walking around with towels is not fitting."

"So shall I just let the guests go without towels when Teresa decides she does not need to show up? What would you suggest? Sometimes I wonder if we will ever get responsible help. It seems to me I remember some fairy tale about me having to do very little work once we got to Belize. The fact is, I'm working harder here than I ever did in New York."

Ludlow cleared his throat. "I know we are still working things out and I so wish you wouldn't have to be doing any of the work. But after only a year and a half in business, we can't really afford anything else."

"I do what needs to be done," Millicent said briefly. "I know that repeat guests and recommendations depend as much on good service as proper accommodations and beautiful surroundings."

Ludlow nodded contentedly. "Sometimes I still can't believe our success. Every weekend we are filled to 80 percent capacity and often during the week at least 50 percent. That is phenomenal for a new motel. Mr. King told me to expect to be in business for at least five years before we begin to show a big profit. We are doing that already."

A broad smile spread across his face. "People in Belize City stop and speak to me when I am in town. Since we opened the office in the city to handle our business, a number of prominent businessmen and politicians recognize me and come out to give our establishment a try."

Millicent gave a small sigh. "They must like what they see because our weekend nights are getting awfully crowded and noisy."

"Oh, yes, they like it." Then looking at his wife and sensing her displeasure, he said defensively, "You know men. They always need a place where they can unwind and just enjoy themselves. People all over the world do that. On Mondays they go back to their work and are ready to face their challenges."

"Back to their wives and children where they should have been," Millicent said, frowning slightly. "They never seem to bring their families; instead, they just bring some flighty girlfriends who hang on their arms and giggle and show off."

"Look, Daddy," Dawn exclaimed, bounding in the door. "I found this little kitten out by the fence, right beside the road. Look at the poor thing. It's scared and hungry." The wee bit of fur opened a pink mouth and let out a silent meow. "Can I keep it?" Dawn begged. "Please, Daddy?"

"Take it away," Ludlow said with a frown. "It is probably riddled with parasites and who knows what else."

Taking the kitten from her daughter's arms, Millicent looked at her husband. "I think having a pet might be good for our daughter," she said firmly. "Dawn has very few friends to play with and this might just be a good time for us to adopt this stray."

"Oh, goody, goody!" Dawn was hopping gleefully from one foot to the other.

Ludlow opened his mouth to protest, but Millicent stared straight into his eyes. "This move down here has not been easy on some of us, Ludlow. Let her keep the kitten."

"I'll get some milk," Dawn yelled as she dashed toward the kitchen.

"Please, Ludlow. Our daughter is lonely."

Dawn had gotten a saucer and poured milk into it. She placed the saucer on the floor and Millicent lowered the tiny kitten beside it. At first the kitten seemed not to know what to do, but when it smelled the milk, the kitten's head lowered and a little pink tongue flicked in and out rapidly.

"It likes the milk," Dawn said with shining eyes. "Oh, Mommy, look how cute it is!"

Ludlow sighed and went out the door. He headed toward the restaurant.

Mrs. Jensen waved, beckoning him to join them at the bar. Her tinkling laugh evaporated into the sunshine.

CHAPTER 10

NEVER ENOUGH

"January 17, 1974, will go down in history," Emory King said, gazing at the infant boy in Ludlow's arms. "This boy is destined for a great position in Belize someday."

The group of prominent businessmen, their wives, and the politicians from Belize City all lifted their glasses and cheered. Ludlow flashed his broad smile at the crowd. He put his free arm around Millicent, and with Dawn standing in front of them, the family posed for photographs.

Ludlow Walker Junior was dressed in white, his skin still damp from the christening water, and his two godfathers flanked the family on opposite sides.

"To the success of Mopan Motel!"

"Long live the Walker legacy!"

"To a wonderful future in Belize for the Walker family!"

The well wishers toasted often and lustily. The bar, filled to capacity, became the scene of increasingly rowdy merrymaking. But Ludlow Junior had had enough. His fretful cries became more demanding, and finally he used his tiny lungs to voice his full-throated disapproval of the festivities going on around him.

"See, he is an orator already, Ludlow," Mr. King laughed loudly, shouting above the cries of the infant.

"Dawn, come. It is time to put this boy to bed." Millicent smiled a farewell and took the children out into the warm night. The afternoon rain had transformed the oppressive tropical air and everything smelled fresh and clean.

"Mommy, I am so glad we have the baby." Dawn stood beside her mother and watched as baby Ludlow opened his tiny mouth and yawned. "He is the cutest baby I ever saw."

Millicent smiled at her eight-year-old daughter and echoed, "Yes, he is cute. I am hoping that our sonny will do a lot for all of us. We are now truly a family because Daddy has always wanted a boy."

"Will Ludlow Junior someday be president of Belize?" Dawn asked, her enormous dark eyes looking at her mother. "I heard a gentleman say that with Daddy's money and our connections to the political world, our baby could someday be president."

Millicent smiled. "Dawn, you get such grown-up ideas. Well, who knows what the future holds for our son? Since he is Belizean by birth, he surely could be a candidate. And if his father has any say in the matter, his son will have no lack of anything he needs to succeed in whatever field he chooses."

The baby stirred in her arms. "But for right now, I just want to cuddle and love him and let him be my baby. Talk about the future is all grand and fine, but right now our son needs love from his family." Looking out into the dark night outside the open window, Millicent was silent for a moment and then repeated, "Love. I am beginning to realize just how important love is and how much we hurt if love fades away."

"I love you, Mommy." Dawn flung her arms around her mother. "I love you more than anyone else!"

Millicent closed her eyes. "I love you too, my sweetie. You will always be my precious daughter."

The music and laughter swelled out into the night. Millicent laid the sleeping infant in his crib and crossed to the open window. She closed the window, shutting out the sounds of the party.

"See what I found on Lot 73."

Millicent looked up to see Goff approach her with an object in his hand. "What is it?" she inquired curiously.

"From the Indian tribe that used to live here," the night watchman answered, stretching out his hand and showing Millicent his find. "Arrow from stick to kill animals. Or to kill people."

The white arrowhead gleamed on Goff's upturned palm. Millicent picked it up and studied it. "My, this is history, Goff. I wonder what all the people who lived here in Belize hundreds of years ago used to do."

"Mostly hunt," Goff replied. "Towns used to be that direction." He waved toward the north. "Many animals were here in the grasslands, so there was good hunting."

Millicent nodded and handed back the artifact. "I wonder if it was lonely back then too," she sighed.

"You lonely?" Goff peered at her. "You don't like it here?"

Millicent sighed again and looked at the laundry bin in front of her. "Goff, I lived in New York City where people are around all the time. I was born and raised there and I went to school there. That is all I knew until we came here," she said, indicating the motel complex with a wave of her hand. "Here, there are people, but they are just customers. I have no friends. The people who live in the development are usually just here on weekends or for vacations. So, who do I know?"

Goff nodded sympathetically. "I have many friends in my town. We sit together evenings. We eat together and party. You are stuck here, working." He looked at the laundry bin.

Millicent sighed. Goff understood her dilemma. He seemed to be the only one who did. Funny, she would never have expected a native Belizean man several decades older than her to become her best friend. But it was true. He was the only one who seemed to understand her.

"You must tell your husband to get more people to work. You should not do this work," Goff said bluntly.

Dawn came out of their living quarters carrying the baby. Ludlow Junior was now two years old, but they still called him the baby. "Bring Pongolon to me!" Goff called, using the nickname the Belizeans had given the young heir.

Ludlow Junior struggled in his sister's arms, and when Dawn set him down, he ran as fast as he could toward his elderly friend. "Yippee!" Goff tossed the boy into the air and the two laughed together. Dawn danced around with glee, laughing and clapping her hands.

Millicent looked at her happy children playing with Goff. Then she glanced at the parking spot where Ludlow's Chevy pickup was parked when he was at the motel. Empty.

Millicent began pushing the cart toward the laundry room. "Here, let me do that," Goff called, setting Ludlow Junior on the ground and pushing her gently aside.

"This is not your job," Millicent protested. "Aren't you ready to go home? Your shift has already ended."

"Doesn't matter. I want to do this for you."

"Ride. Pongo want ride." Ludlow Junior was clamoring for attention. Strong arms set the boy on top of the laundry, and with shouts of laughter from the children, the cart went racing across the courtyard. Millicent followed wearily.

"Come along with me to the restaurant," Ludlow suggested, buttoning his colorful shirt. "Dawn can watch the baby tonight."

Millicent folded a towel and added it to the stack on the bed. "I'm too tired," she protested. "You go on."

"Just for a while. You can always slip away later," Ludlow persisted. "You hardly ever show up at the restaurant in the evenings. Please come. Dress up and have a night with us."

"Ludlow, I told you I'm tired. I have been up since early this morning managing the house, taking care of Junior, taking Dawn to and from school, not to mention cleaning up the mess those people left at the party last night. I need to rest."

"You could just sit in a chair and have a nice drink," Ludlow continued, looking at his reflection in the mirror and dashing his face with cologne. "You could rest there."

Millicent rolled her eyes and said firmly, "To me, rest means lying down on a bed and trying to sleep, not sitting in a chair at a loud party trying to appear happy."

"You work too much," Ludlow said absentmindedly, slipping into his sandals.

"I agree," Millicent said in even tones. "I have been saying so for the last three years. At last you agree."

Ludlow glanced quickly at his wife.

"I have been asking for help," Millicent continued. "You always say we can't afford it just yet. You need to pay off this motel. Ludlow, I know we are making good money. Why are we driving ourselves so hard? Why are you constantly away from home, looking into other investments? Always at the office, chasing important people in order to advance your political interests and hobnobbing with all the rich and important. Is this the life you want?" Millicent suddenly found a voice for all that had been bottled up for a long time.

"Why, Millicent, I had no idea . . ."

"Of course you had no idea; you are not here most of the time. Your children are growing up and you hardly spend time with them. I am lonely and hardly have any friends. Do you know who my closest friend is?" Millicent glared at her husband. "Goff."

Ludlow's mouth opened in amazement. "Goff?" he echoed. "The night watchman! That old man?"

"He listens to me when I want to talk. He plays with the children. We talk."

"Millicent, you are tired and your nerves need a rest. Go take a nice bath and go to bed. I can stop by and ask your mother to come over for the evening. You are her favorite daughter. She moved down here to be close to you and the children. I would have thought you would say she is your closest friend. And what about Mrs. Sansom? She is always coming over. She could be your friend." Ludlow eased himself out the door. "Do you want me to ask your mother to come?"

Millicent shook her head and sat down on the bed. With a wave of her hand she motioned him to leave.

He didn't understand. He had no clue what she was talking about. And suddenly, Millicent didn't really care to attempt an explanation. It never helped to try to tell him what she was feeling. He always suggested ridiculous solutions, like thinking she could be a friend with that Sansom woman. It was disgustingly obvious why their neighbor was always at the bar when Ludlow was present. She never seemed to come when the Chevy truck was not in its usual parking space.

No, she did not want her mother. She did not want to listen to someone who agreed with her, someone who saw what was happening to their marriage. She did not need to hear aloud the words that were silently pounding in her brain.

Millicent wept into her pillow. Outside, life seemed like paradise to the many guests who stayed in the rooms, partied at the bar, and danced to the music. But inside, Millicent felt trapped. Trapped in a country she had never gotten used to. Trapped in a life that seemed to become more and more of a drudgery every day. And yes, even trapped in a loveless marriage.

"Seafront property is something I want to look into," Ludlow told the real estate agent. "I am beginning to see that the motels on the coast are more popular every year. Even though I offer wonderful accommodations and good food and drinks, just last weekend I was at the coast and met some of my former guests. I need oceanfront property to build a new motel."

"You are a wise man," Mr. Tallon said suavely. "You seem to have the gift of knowing when to move on. Now the ten-acre site I have listed here is not far from the airport and would be perfect for such a venture." He spread out the survey map on the table. "See, you would have all this ocean frontage. The beach here is perfect for sunbathing and swimming. There is ample room back here for your hotel."

Ludlow felt his excitement growing. This would be an outlet for the restlessness he felt growing inside him. He wanted success. He wanted prestige. He wanted the best that life could offer him.

He used to be satisfied with the achievements he had gained. Rising to prominence in the Merchant Marines had given him a sense of what he could do if he really tried. Now, the success that Mopan Motel had achieved was another sign of his ability to succeed with an enterprise that had only been a dream at one time. It was time to plan bigger, to have more scope for his imagination, to aim for the stars.

"I want to investigate several other possible sites," Ludlow told the agent. "I want to make sure I get the very best possible place to build my hotel."

"There is some more land available farther up the coast," Mr. Tallon said eagerly. "Why don't we make an appointment to drive up there? How about tomorrow? What time?"

"Ah, let me see." Ludlow checked his appointment book. "How about ten o'clock? I should be free at ten."

The two shook hands and Ludlow left. He felt the familiar rush of adrenaline course through him. More and bigger investments, that was what he wanted. Life was good. Nice little family. Good contacts. Successful motel business. The sun really did shine brightly on him in Belize.

Ludlow's thoughts drifted back to his boyhood in Jamaica. He saw himself in the stuffy auto parts store and then adventuring into a career on the ships. He had been back to Jamaica to sell his lots and see his family. His father had passed away, but his mother and Gerald and Joy were always glad to see him.

He had done well in New York City too. From washing dishes to working two airline jobs to investing in Wall Street, he had sweated his way to success. He had also taken risks in buying property and then moving on to investments here in Belize. His shrewd choices had paid off. Yes, life was good, and he was only in his early forties, ready to take on new challenges and conquer new frontiers.

"But—we can't afford to have you go," Ludlow objected later that afternoon. "I . . . we don't have the money on hand."

"I am going to my father's funeral, Ludlow Walker," Millicent insisted through her tears. "My mother agreed to go with me."

"Your mother? She doesn't even like your father," Ludlow said incredulously.

"I said she is going with me. Ludlow, you know what? You are so wrapped up in your life down here that you don't even know what is going on. Belize is your life, but it is not mine. My father died! Don't you understand?" Tears continued to roll down her cheeks.

"But you haven't seen him for years. Why is this so important to you?"

Millicent continued packing. "No, you wouldn't understand. You have an empty space where most people have a heart."

"My heart is in Belize. This is my home. I left the other places and here is where I belong. I will be buried here—many years from now."

"Buried, that is how I feel in this place. Buried and trapped," Millicent said, moving briskly about. "Dorcas will take care of the children during the day, and I guess you can take care of them at night or make other arrangements. Now, are you going to take us to the airport, or shall I call a taxi?"

"But, Millicent, tomorrow I am to meet with the real estate agent and look at some property. It's right on the beach . . ." Ludlow's voice trailed off as his wife fixed him with a frigid stare.

"One minute you tell me I can't afford to go to my father's funeral in New York and the next you tell me you want to invest in beachfront land? Ludlow, are you crazy? Now please get ready and take me to the airport." Tears began streaming down Millicent's cheeks again.

Ludlow shook his head and left the room. He would never understand women.

CHAPTER 11

AN UNRAVELING MARRIAGE

"We are going back to the States to visit my mother," Millicent told Ludlow. "She is not coming back to Belize, and she wants us to come and stay with her."

"What about me?" Ludlow asked, his voice rising. "What will I do without my family?"

"Look for profitable investments," Millicent replied calmly but bluntly. "Look after your money family."

"That's not fair," Ludlow protested. "You know I care about you and the children. Don't I provide you with a home and food and all the clothes you want?" Millicent did not answer. She sighed and went into the bedroom, closing the door behind her.

The telephone rang.

"Mr. Walker? This is Mr. Tallon. I just had to tell you that right on the coast there is a new five-acre tract of land that has just come on the market. This is the nicest piece of land I have seen yet. Beautiful sandy beach, easy access to the highway. You will not want this to slip away from you." The voice on the other end of the telephone spoke persuasively.

"I will come meet you right away," Ludlow said. "I am free at the moment." He replaced the telephone and turned around. No one was in sight. He heard voices inside Dawn's bedroom, and then the back door swung open.

"Pongolon!" Ludlow greeted his three-year-old son. "Daddy is going away for several hours. You be the man of the family now."

"Go with you," Ludlow Junior suggested quickly, his dark eyes lighting up.

"Not this time. I might be gone most of the day," Ludlow told his son. "I will take you the next time I go to Belize City." He always loved taking his son with him whenever he went to his office, showing off his heir and son to all the people in the city.

Ludlow Junior shrugged his shoulders diplomatically and turned and scampered outside. "Goff, wait!" he yelled as he saw the watchman cross the compound. "Pongolon is coming with you."

Knocking on the closed door, Ludlow called loudly, "I am going out for several hours." There was no answer, so Ludlow took his briefcase and left.

It was after dark when he returned home. The property had indeed proved promising. Ludlow and Mr. Tallon had spent the entire afternoon walking the property, measuring distances, and planning where the best place would be for the hotel, the parking area, and the restaurant. They had even found the perfect spot for the tennis courts on a knoll overlooking the ocean.

The house was quiet and dark. "Hello, I'm home," Ludlow called.

All was still. The music from the bar at the other end of the building played on and on. For some reason, the shrill voice of the female soloist irritated Ludlow as he waited for an answer to his greeting. He snapped on a light. Everything was neat and orderly.

Then he saw it. A simple white piece of paper, folded in thirds, lay on the dining room table. Even as he reached for it, Ludlow felt a cold fear squeeze at his heart. His long fingers trembled slightly as he unfolded the paper.

Ludlow,

I have taken the children with me to Miami to visit my mother. There is food in the refrigerator and your laundry is clean and in the drawers.

—Millicent

Ludlow stared at the short message. He read it again. Then, feeling a hot surge of anger flood over him, he slapped the paper onto the table and stalked to the kitchen. Turning on the cold water full force, he washed his hands. He dried them on the towel and went back into the dining room and picked up the letter again. Once more he read it. It still bore the same terrible message.

Slowly, and with clenched teeth, Ludlow crumpled the paper and crushed it into a ball. He threw it on the floor. Pulling out a chair, he crumpled onto the seat and bent forward, resting his head in his hands.

His thoughts raced wildly. How could she do this to him? Who would see that the rooms were clean and ready for the guests? Fred was the manager, but it was always Millicent who made the final check and put out extra towels. It was his wife who kept the motel looking fresh and clean, arranging flowers for the vases and keeping the refrigerator stocked with fruit juices. Who would do that now?

That's the first thing you would think of. He could almost hear Millicent's voice, tinged with sadness, in his brain. *My contribution to your business is really what you will miss the most.*

"No!" Ludlow declared out loud in the empty room. "That's just not true."

In spite of his declaration, a small voice in his conscience quietly insisted that indeed it was true.

"I need my wife. I need my children," Ludlow looked up and spoke to the ceiling.

Well, he reasoned to himself after a few moments. *They just left for a visit. They will be back. Come on, I need a drink and some social life. I'll go over to the bar and spend my evenings there. There are other people who are always glad to see me.*

Ludlow got up swiftly. He needed to get out of the empty house and seek companionship. Loneliness and fear must not be allowed to creep into his soul.

On the way down the hall, he turned on the light in their bedroom. Everything was neat and tidy. Ludlow Junior's crib was in the corner, but there was no teddy bear waiting to spend the night with the young boy.

The crib looked empty—cold and sterile. No dark head was lying asleep on the little pillow and no rumpled blanket covered a small form.

Ludlow slapped the wall with the flat of his hand. Turning abruptly, he snapped off the light and flung the door shut. Swearing under his breath, he left the house and hurried across the compound to the bar where lights, music, and reckless laughter floated out into the night.

"You heard yet when Mrs. Walker and the children are returning?" Goff intercepted Ludlow and Emory King as they left their vehicle and went toward the bar.

"No, I haven't," Ludlow said shortly, scowling slightly at his watchman.

Then, indicating with his head toward the pool, he said sharply, "Goff, I asked you to fix that break in the fence. It still isn't done."

The two men walked on and Goff at first wrinkled his brow in puzzlement. Then he shook his head. This was the first he had ever been told to fix the fence. Something was obviously bothering Mr. Walker.

"I don't think Millicent liked it much here," Emory said bluntly. "Something tells me she might not be back."

"What?" Ludlow cut in, refusing to face the thought that haunted his own mind. "Of course she'll be back. She just went to visit. Millicent has always been her mother's favorite daughter. She knows I love her, and I've got to have the children back. I miss Pongolon like crazy."

"I've lived a long time and I've seen a lot of things," the elderly man said knowingly.

"You're joking. Come on, I think you need a stiff drink."

Emory raised one eyebrow and said nothing. He had seen the signs—the signs a man simply will not see in his own marriage, but which are so glaringly obvious to the rest of the world.

"What can I get you, Mr. Walker?" Josephine's voice was accompanied by a bright smile. "Do you want me to concoct something new for you? I guarantee you will like it."

Ludlow looked at his new bartender fondly. Josephine was a treasure, as he had quickly seen that evening when he had stopped at the café where she had worked in the city. He had not hesitated long before inviting her to work at Mopan for better wages. "Plus, there are many other benefits with the job as well," he had told her with a wink.

"I have heard that line many times before." Josephine had been suspicious of his motives at first.

"Come and try it. You can always leave if you don't like it," Ludlow had told her with a smile. And so she had come, and neither of them had regretted the arrangement. "Something new," Ludlow now said, settling himself onto a stool. "Will you create something new for Mr. King as well?"

Josephine cocked her head sideways for a moment. "Something different . . . each man needs to have a custom-mixed drink that suits his character and temperament." The men laughed.

"Now mixing drinks is becoming a skill that only character analysts can perfect," Ludlow laughed, eager to enter into the game. "Bring it on."

Josephine pulled levers, mixed flavors, filled glasses, sniffed appreciatively, rolled her eyes upward in delight at some, and shook her head disdainfully at others. Finally, with a flourish, she set a glass mug in front of Ludlow.

He sipped appreciatively, keeping his eye on the girl watching him. The tangy drink slid smoothly down his throat. He opened his eyes wide in delight and pretended to swoon sideways. "Wow! You do know your drinks!"

They all laughed together.

"You seem to be forgetting me," Emory protested, trying to look dejected.

Josephine leaned forward and peered into Emory's eyes. "I know just the thing. All the time I was fixing Mr. Walker's drink, I was wondering what I would make for his fine friend. Now I know."

"Hey, Josephine, quit this Mr. Walker thing. My name is Ludlow."

"Oh, but I only call my close friends by their first name. You are my boss, Mr. Walker," she pretended to be serious and businesslike.

"Just forget I am your boss, Josephine. Now, say my name," he urged.

"Ludlow," Josephine cooed with a smile.

"I like to hear you say that," Ludlow said softly.

Emory rolled his eyes. "My drink," he said loudly and muttered something under his breath.

No one seemed to hear him.

"When can we eat?" Josephine's voice broke petulantly into Ludlow's sleep. "I'm getting hungry."

Ludlow grunted and dozed off again. The umbrella shaded him from the Mexican sun beside the motel pool and his body craved sleep. They had been up too long the night before.

Josephine pushed him. "When do we go to eat?" she asked again.

Ludlow sighed. This girl was taking too much for granted. Vacations in Mexico, new clothes, and expensive jewelry. He was getting tired of her demands.

This pattern was repeating itself all too often. At first, the girls seemed so pliable and grateful for his gifts and surprise trips, but soon they became demanding and possessive. Yes, it was time to let Josephine go. There would be others to replace her.

Millicent,

When are you coming home and bringing the children? It has been three months since you left and I want you to come back. Dawn needs to go back to school or she will miss too many classes. And Ludlow Junior will need to be here to keep in touch with everyone here. Goff asks about you.

The motel is busy and I need your help. There are so many things that need to be done.

Please, Millicent, come back.

Your husband,

Ludlow

Millicent stood in her mother's apartment reading the letter. She shook her head and put the letter with the others on top of her dresser.

Each letter was shorter than the previous one, but they all contained the same message. Come back, there is work to be done. Come back for the children's sake.

Barbara walked into her daughter's bedroom. "Another letter from Ludlow?" she asked sharply, looking at Millicent's face.

Expecting no answer, she continued, "Millicent, face it. That man is not going to give up trying to get you and the children back to Belize. You need to tell him that you are making a life for yourself here where you belong. Did you tell him Dawn is in school and Junior is enrolled in daycare?"

Millicent stood beside the dresser looking at nothing in particular. She shook her head in answer to her mother's questions. "I don't write to him so, no, he doesn't know."

"Then write and tell him. Let him know what kind of husband he is, letting you come up here with almost no money, hunting for a job and never getting any support from him. He owes you child support."

Millicent allowed her mother's words to wash over her without protest. They were nothing new, just the regular litany of complaints repeated over and over again.

"Bye, Mom. Bye, Grandma," Dawn called as she headed out the door, her school bag over her shoulder.

"Dawn, do you want to go back to Belize?" Barbara asked loudly, looking shrewdly at Millicent.

"Never! Even if Mom goes back, I'm staying here. I hate Belize," Dawn said with passion, stamping her foot. She flung herself out the door and the apartment shuddered with the force of the slamming door.

"Mother! I wish you wouldn't bring the children into this . . . this . . ."

"This one-sided fight?" Barbara finished cuttingly. "You know it would never work for you to return. You would simply go back to working for a man who never appreciated you, and you would work like a slave. I saw all the work you did when I lived there. He can afford to invest in land and has money to spend on himself, but when it comes to hiring someone to work for you, he is stingy and you know it. Now, see, you are not there and yet the motel is going on. If he has to make do without you, he can."

"Oh, Mom, don't," Millicent held her head. "I have to get ready for work and I don't want another headache to make it hard to concentrate." She shook her head. "I just wish all this would go away. I want to be free from stress."

Glancing at the pill bottle on Millicent's dresser, Barbara said, "Your blood pressure is up again, isn't it? Listen. You get yourself a good lawyer and file for divorce. Get him out of your life." The older woman left the bedroom.

With a groan Millicent sat on her bed. She reviewed the last letter mentally once more. It had no mention of love, not one word of endearment. Only that she was needed and that he missed the children.

Where was the Ludlow of their courtship? She recalled the tender endearments, the flowers, the gifts, the dinners in romantic restaurants. She was always so proud of his good looks, his tall form, and impeccable manners. When did all this start? Millicent retraced their married years.

Maybe she should never have insisted that he leave his position in the Merchant Marines and get a job in New York City. It seemed that once Ludlow began working, he couldn't stop. During the first years of marriage he had worked those double shifts, and when money started flowing, he just invested more time in pursuing riches.

If she was honest, Millicent knew she had enjoyed the nice things of life that money could buy. But what was all that worth now? She was almost penniless, dependent on her mother for a place to live, had a job that hardly paid enough to keep herself and her children in clothes, and yet, for some reason, she actually enjoyed her life now more than she had for the last five years.

"To live with someone when love is gone is worse than living by yourself and not having to be reminded of what you once had," she said to herself in a whisper. "Oh, Ludlow, where have we missed it?"

With a sigh, she stood up. Yes, she would go see a lawyer. She needed to put all this behind her and make a life for herself and the children.

Checking herself in the mirror, she noted the worry line creasing her forehead. She smoothed it out with one hand and tried to smile at her reflection, but she knew the manufactured smile was merely pasted on her face. The smile was gone from her heart.

June 15, 1979

Mr. Ludlow Walker,

Notice is hereby served to one, Ludlow Walker, of a certain action taken by Mrs. Millicent Walker to file for a divorce on the grounds of irreconcilable differences.

Ludlow did not read the rest of the legal jargon. One word leaped off the page and burned itself into his brain. Divorce. Millicent was filing for divorce.

Ludlow breathed heavily. He stared bleakly out the window of his pickup. Turning the key in the ignition, he drove away from the post office and through the crowded streets of Belize City. An elderly man, slowly making his way across in front of him, leaned heavily on his cane.

Irritated at the delay, Ludlow slammed the brake, leaned out the window, and yelled, "Get out of the way!" as he blew his horn.

Yanking his steering wheel to the left, he stomped on the gas, ignoring the yell of the pedestrians, and tore down the road. His blood boiled as he sped out of the city and onto the highway toward Hattieville, where the government had erected barracks to shelter the hurricane victims who had lost their homes.

How could she do this to him? How could she take the children from him and live with her mother? It was probably all Barbara Dennings' fault. She never had liked him. She didn't want Millicent to marry him. Probably wanted her to marry that Cecil.

"Cecil," Ludlow snorted. "Simpering little sneak."

What about Ludlow Junior? He was supposed to be groomed for an important office here in Belize. Ludlow cringed at the thought of what would happen to his public image when the news got out that his wife was divorcing him.

Even though he knew he had been unfaithful to Millicent, it still hurt to think that she was rejecting him. His brain would not listen to his heart telling him that she must have felt wounded by his rejection as well.

His ego smarted. His wife was divorcing him.

He slowed down as he came to the Hattieville crossroads with the police station strategically located at the junction. Turning right, he sailed past the mission house the Mennonites had built to help the hurricane victims.

Good people, the Mennonites were. Hardworking, not afraid of getting right down into the daily lives of the refugees and helping them get back on their feet. *A lot of work for nothing,* Ludlow often thought as he watched them labor for years trying to help the shiftless idlers and drunks. But, their labors were fruitful with others. They had a little church and many of the Belizeans attended. They even had several of their own local pastors.

A cluster of people buying chicken stood in front of a small building. Ah, there was Miss Nancy, selling her butchered chickens. Recognizing Ludlow's truck, the middle-aged woman lifted her hand and hailed him. She wore her long dress and her usual white veiling, and her ready smile was as warm as always. Even in his foul mood, Ludlow felt a spot of cheer come into his otherwise dry soul. He waved and tooted the horn at his friend.

Yes, Miss Nancy was his friend. At first he was just a customer, glad to have a dependable place where he could buy quality chicken for his motel. But as the months and years went by, he found himself actually enjoying his visits with this pleasant woman.

Nice lives they had, those Mennonites. Peaceful, seemingly content with what was given them, they hardly let anything ruffle their orderly lives. For some reason Ludlow found himself almost envying them today. They sure did without a lot of stuff, he knew. They never seemed to be at the festivals and never, never would they come to his bar. Way too religious for that.

Every so often they had meetings in their churches for a week at a time, and he had heard reports of people becoming religious and joining their church. Even the Belizean women changed their clothes and dressed in long skirts and put white veils on their black hair. Yes, the Mennonites were strange people, but something about them piqued his interest.

But now was not a time to think about the Mennonites. Ludlow had to deal with the fact that Millicent wanted a divorce, and she was going to get one. He slammed his fist against the steering wheel and swore. The pain that shot up his arm was satisfying. Something else besides his heart should share the pain.

All right then. Let her go ahead. See if he cared. He could always get another woman. There were plenty of girls around who loved his attention.

What about his children? Would they grow up without their father? Would Dawn even miss him? And Ludlow Junior . . .

Ludlow pulled his truck to the side of the road and stopped the engine. He felt his body sag against the truck seat as the image of his little son swam in front of him. Pongolon. How could he bear giving him up? Hot, silent tears coursed down his cheeks as Ludlow felt despair wash over him.

The scrubby fields on each side of the road were empty, and in the distance two figures walked slowly off into the horizon. No one seemed to care about the lonely, disappointed man sitting in his truck, tasting the bitterness of divorce. The hot sun shone down on the land that had once seemed so promising, so like paradise. Now it seemed to offer only an empty, lonely tunnel into a joyless future.

CHAPTER 12

STILL SEARCHING

The parking lot of Mopan Motel was filled to capacity and the music played haunting Caribbean melodies, inviting the listeners to give in to the languid atmosphere that permeated the compound. It was not yet noon and many of the guests were still in their rooms, but the early risers were at the cocktail lounge drinking coffee and planning for the day.

"Yes, I plan to sell Mopan." Ludlow turned to face the man beside him at the bar. "I have signed documents of intent to purchase oceanfront property, and I plan to build the best seaside hotel in Belize. Ben, I want your opinion."

Ben Feinstein carefully sipped his steaming mug of coffee. The many gold rings glittering on his hands spoke of wealth and shrewd investments.

Ludlow admired his Jewish friend. "We are brothers," he had once remarked to Ben. "My grandfather was a Jew, so that gives me enough Jewish blood to claim kinship, doesn't it?"

Ben had laughed and replied, "I am a brother to anyone who is successful in business and enterprises; so I say, yes, we are brothers, not only by blood, but also by nature."

Now Ben glanced briefly at Ludlow; then he looked around the lounge. His observant eyes took in the well-stocked bar, the tastefully decorated lounge, and the wealthy patrons at the table. Then he looked at Ludlow again.

"I am not sure how the economic winds are blowing right now at the beginning of 1981. I am concerned about some signs I've seen of a soft-ening economy." He tapped a finger on the counter slowly, the turquoise ring moving up and down in a serious fashion.

"What do you mean?" Ludlow did not want his idea stalled, and yet he knew his friend as a savvy businessman and really wanted his opinion.

"Look," Ben said bluntly, "other hotels and guest houses are already on the oceanfront. If there are too many hotels and accommodations, the business will be spread out among the many until the tourists come by the thousands. It will take time for you to gain a reputation. Until then, you could get hit financially. If the international economy does suffer, you will be the first to feel it as tourists stop traveling. Belize is still a developing country, not to mention that it is prone to hurricanes and tropical storms."

The two men were silent as they drank their coffee. Ludlow knew he should carefully consider Ben's advice. Too much hinged on the decision he was facing.

"Well, I can put Mopan up for sale and see what happens," Ludlow said finally. "A good motel like mine should not be hard to sell. Almost every week someone comes up to me and asks about investment property in Belize. Many of the women speak enthusiastically about buying here and retiring in our country."

"Until the storms hit and the weather reaches 110 degrees in the sum-mer," Ben said caustically. "You know those are merely illusionary dreams of an earthly paradise."

Ludlow laughed. "Good word picture. But it doesn't hurt to perpetrate those dreams if it brings in money."

More guests came in as noon approached. Ludlow greeted them with his ready, made-for-guests smile. Most of the people stopped to chat with him and tell him how they enjoyed this place. When there was a lull, Ludlow looked at Ben and raised his left eyebrow, "Well?"

"Don't expect an immediate sale," Ben told him bluntly. He shrugged his shoulder expressively.

"Say! I'll auction Mopan! That way I can have immediate cash to in-vest in the other property. I can move right ahead after the details have been worked out with the new owner," Ludlow said gleefully as he sat up straight, pleased with his inspiration.

"Hmm," Ben said noncommittally.

"I'll advertise on the radio and in the newspapers for several months. I might even advertise in some places in the States. Some eager investor will want a thriving business. I have all my records to confirm my earnings," Ludlow said as he rubbed his hands together in excitement. "Come on, have a drink on the house."

"Now this will be contingent on the sale of Mopan, of course," Ludlow told Mr. Tallon. "I won't be able to go ahead with any purchase of land until I free some of my equity. I also put the 103-acre tract up for sale, but I don't have any offers yet. It seems like the market has slowed in real estate. What is your analysis?"

"There are still buyers looking," Mr. Tallon said, trying to sound optimistic. "Perhaps they're more cautious, but there is still a lot of money people need to invest. Several businessmen from Germany were here last week to look at possibilities."

"Tell them about Mopan," Ludlow urged. "The auction date is set for March 8 of this year, and if they would know about it, they might want to come back to bid on it."

"Yes, sir!" Mr. Tallon was as excited as his client. He knew that if Ludlow sold Mopan Motel, he would be eager to buy the land on the ocean, which would mean a hefty commission for himself.

"It will be a first class hotel," Ludlow said again. "I have all my ideas on paper and after Mopan sells, I will submit them to an architect. Remember that knoll? Instead of building the tennis courts there, I want an exclusive clubhouse overlooking the ocean. There will be a cocktail lounge in the hotel, but I want an opulent one for private parties on that spot." In his mind Ludlow saw the magnificent building becoming an icon for his new project.

"Look, you contact those Germans. I have had several inquiries into the financial status of Mopan, and I am looking forward to a large crowd of bidders," Ludlow predicted exultantly.

This new project was becoming an obsession with him. It gave him something to dream about, a purpose for his otherwise purposeless life. So many times lately he felt jaded, washed-up, and listless. There were times when he really felt as though his life was over. Millicent and the children were gone, his current girlfriend was getting tiresome, and he needed something new to bolster himself. Perhaps this new dream would do it.

"All right, ladies and gentlemen, we have here one of the best commercial properties in all of Belize." The auctioneer looked over the small group of people in the cocktail lounge. Several well-dressed men were there and a number of guests from the motel. Ludlow was dressed in his business suit, smoothing the creases in his trousers with nervous fingers. He scanned the faces of the onlookers. Who would be the bidders?

The small size of the crowd had at first bothered him. Maybe he shouldn't have chosen a Sunday for the date of the auction. Perhaps a Friday or a Saturday would have been better. But businessmen were not going to stay away from an opportunity even if it meant skipping church. That is, if they ever attended church.

"The financial records have been supplied by Mr. Ludlow Walker, whom many of you know as one of the finest men in our country. He has brought prosperity and commerce to our area, and we are indeed grateful for his vision and enterprise." The auctioneer nodded toward Ludlow.

"We all know what a fine motel Mopan has been for the last . . . how many years, Mr. Walker?"

"Ten years," Ludlow smiled and nodded.

"Now, ladies and gentlemen, that is a long time. A proven record for any establishment, and as you can see, there is not a finer establishment than this. This motel is in a prime location: not far from Belize City and right next to Mr. Emory King and Mr. Ludlow Walker's development of Tropical Park, one of the most prestigious developments in all Belize." The auctioneer continued his sales pitch with enthusiasm.

"This desirable property consists of seven acres and twenty-three units, a caretaker or owner's unit (where Mr. Walker currently resides), fully furnished suites, this cocktail lounge, an efficient staff eager to stay on and serve the new owners, and dependable guests who have been coming here for years." The auctioneer nodded toward the guests watching the auction and then addressed the group. "So, what am I to bid for Mopan Motel? What is the opening bid for this fine establishment, all ready to produce income for your investment?"

Silence fell over the crowd. Several curious onlookers scanned the faces of the people, but Ludlow looked only at the auctioneer. He felt his heart pound rapidly.

"Now, ladies and gentlemen," the auctioneer's voice broke into the silence, "you all know that Mopan, like I said before, is an excellent choice for investors. We are here today, offering the real estate, the furnishings, and a financially sound business. Come now, place your bids."

Several people shifted, a few murmured among themselves, and then once more an awkward silence filled the room.

Ludlow felt the palms of his hands sweat. He smoothed them against his trousers and continued to watch the auctioneer.

Scanning the crowd for any sign of a bid, the auctioneer tried again. "Well, I know this is a large investment, but we are willing to begin with any amount. Just submit your bid and we will take the auction from there. We are looking for a bid on Mopan Motel and we welcome anyone to begin the bidding process."

The advertisements had been published, the announcements made on the radio stations of Belize City, and many of Ludlow's acquaintances had spoken to him about his intentions of selling Mopan. But none of those people were here today. What was happening? Why were there no bidders?

The silence stretched into an enormous cavity that began to envelop Ludlow's hopes and dash them into bits. Tensing his ears to hear any bid, yet feeling a fountain of despair rising up inside, Ludlow found himself taking deep, slow breaths as nothing happened.

The auctioneer's eyes kept darting around from face to face. This was most unusual. What was going on?

As the silence became unbearable, the auctioneer finally said in a deflated voice, "Well, ladies and gentlemen, if any parties are interested in purchasing Mopan, you may speak to me or to Mr. Walker about your intentions." With a dismissing nod, he walked over to Ludlow.

"There may be someone who wanted anonymity." He tried to bolster his words with a smile, but to Ludlow, it was scant hope. "I will mingle with the crowd and speak with them. You stay right here and be available to answer any questions."

Ludlow wanted to get away from all the eyes looking in his direction. Something huge and hollow was opening up in his chest, right where he thought his heart was. He continued to breathe deeply, but even the air he drew into his lungs did not seem to bring any life to his starving system. He felt humiliated and devastated, his grand dreams for the future slipping from his grasp.

When he finally mustered courage to look up, he found himself almost alone. The small group of people had left, leaving the cocktail lounge empty except for Teresa, the bar maid and his current girlfriend. She kept her eyes on her hands as she went on wiping the clean countertop with her dishcloth.

"Ludlow, you want something to drink?" Her voice was tinged with pity.

Ludlow shook his head. The auctioneer came back inside and offered his regrets before leaving. Ludlow stumbled to his chair beside the window and lowered himself to his seat. He was keenly aware of the soft cushion of his chair. For some reason every little detail was suddenly of great importance. He looked at the fabric of his suit and noticed how the threads were woven together. He studied his idle hands lying on his lap.

His fingernails were trimmed and neat. His long fingers were slightly curved, and for some reason he saw himself on board the cargo ship, using his hands to steer the ship through the ocean waters. An intense longing to feel the ship's smooth wheel under the control of his capable hands swept over him.

A feeling of power had always thrilled him as he steered the gigantic vessel through the sea from one port to another. He had always enjoyed the satisfaction that position had given him, the feeling of controlling something big and powerful.

His thoughts drifted to his marriage to Millicent, his days and months and years of working two jobs, investing and speculating and becoming a wealthy man. He thought of Dawn and Ludlow Junior, and of how his hands had made Mopan a success. He remembered how he felt when Millicent took the children and left. He remembered the initial pain when he had been served the divorce papers. That was when he began to experience the panic of a life spiraling out of control. But he had endured. He had thrown himself into his businesses and devoted his time and energy to making a huge success. But all at once, in less than an hour, something had happened. He had lost control. He was now a washed-up, useless man, unable to create the future he had dreamed of.

Where were his friends who liked to come out and spend weekends with him, away from their families and with pretty girls hanging on their arms, drinking his alcoholic drinks and continually slapping him on his shoulders and congratulating him on his keen business sense? Where were the politicians who had assured Ludlow they would always support him? Why did they not bring prospective buyers?

Was there some huge conspiracy against him? Ludlow felt the loneliness of abandonment add itself to his depression. Leaning forward, he groaned aloud, holding his head in his hands. Life held no attraction to him anymore. All he had worked for was gone. No wife, no children, no friends.

That he still had Mopan meant nothing to him now. Even if it continued to make money, just the fact that there were no buyers for it meant he could not go ahead with his plans for the oceanfront hotel. All the grandiose schemes that had so excited him must now be put away.

He lifted his head and saw a few guests wander in and order drinks at the bar. Suddenly he felt an aversion to everything. He wished everyone would leave. He wanted to be alone, but he could not make himself go back to his living quarters. It would be empty in the middle of the day. No wife, no children. He hated this life. He glared almost fiercely at the guests and frowned. Why were they here? What business did they have to come in and order drinks as though everything were normal?

He looked at Teresa. Suddenly he was filled with loathing for her. She laughed at something someone said and the laugh sounded hollow, shallow, and forced. How could she be laughing? She had no right to laugh when his world was falling apart all around him. He clenched his hands tightly. He felt as though he would explode. Something was happening again inside his heart—or the place where his heart had been.

He thought of his mother, still in Jamaica. He had not seen her for years. He wondered what Gerald and Joy were doing. A vision of the mango tree in the neighbor's yard flitted through his mind. All of a sudden he longed for his childhood. Everything had been predictable and orderly. When at home, he had been responsible to his parents. When at school, he had been under the authority and direction of the Anglican teachers.

He thought of the fretting and chafing he had always felt when he was told what to do and what not to do. It had seemed so confining; now it seemed so safe. The world in which he now lived was unstable and frightening. A world he had made with his own brain and strength, but a world that was no longer real.

The empty, aching feeling inside him grew larger and larger until he wondered how there was any space left for his organs. He continued to breathe deeply, trying to grasp hold of something . . . anything that would make sense.

The feeling he had when Millicent divorced him was back, increased ten-fold. Suddenly he felt much older than his forty-four years, washed-up, wrung out by life and discarded as useless. As tears welled up in his eyes, he felt the pressure inside explode. He gave a dry, choking sob.

Teresa looked at him in horror. The guests, holding their drinks, got up and began edging toward the door. Was the owner of Mopan losing his mind?

CHAPTER 13

GOING CRAZY?

Only once in his life had Ludlow felt anything like the hopelessness of this moment. As he sat in the cocktail lounge, he remembered when his mother had called him to come home to Jamaica. His father was dying.

By the time Ludlow arrived, his father had already passed away. He had attended the funeral in the same Anglican church he used to attend as a boy. The liturgies were the same, the formal setting just as he remembered.

But the feeling had not come at the funeral. It was not until afterward when he was helping his mother and siblings go through their father's personal belongings. "I'll keep this," Ludlow had said, holding his father's Bible in his hand and reading the familiar signature on the inside cover. "I didn't even know he had a Bible."

"Yes, you take it," his mother had said, glancing at her oldest son meaningfully. Gerald and Joy had brushed off the memento without a comment. They had not been interested.

While he had been holding his father's Bible, he had glimpsed the emptiness of his life. Back then he still had his family and his wealth was continuing to grow. But just for a moment time had stopped for him, and he had a strange sense that this life was not all there was to living.

Now, as he leaned forward and groaned aloud, he remembered that Bible. Where was it? Dimly he remembered seeing it since they had moved to Belize. It had been in a box with several other items from his youth.

"Find your father's Bible."

Ludlow looked up sharply. Who had spoken to him?

Teresa was still polishing the counter. A few people had wandered in and, after giving him a curious glance, were trying to decide what to order for their Sunday afternoon drinks.

"Your father's Bible. Get it."

The Voice was not audible to anyone else. Ludlow was sure of that. It came from somewhere inside him. *I don't know where it is,* he found himself mentally answering the command.

Silence.

Ludlow felt his heart pound faster. He began questioning whether he had actually heard anything. *Probably just something that came over me because I am so distraught,* he thought. *Besides, what could the Bible do to help me in my situation?*

Again, nothing. There was only silence inside his heart.

Did the Bible really have answers? Was there anything in that book that could help him? The Bible was history, wasn't it? Just a bunch of old stories about brave men and lions and a huge ark and stuff like that. And, of course, stories about Jesus, who claimed to be God. How was that possible?

Pulling up dim memories from his boyhood, Ludlow remembered the Anglican teachers talking about the people in the Bible. David—wasn't he the Jewish king who wrote all those songs? Psalms, they were called.

Ludlow had memorized Bible verses along with the rest of his class. At the time, the words had meant little or nothing to him as he stumbled over passages. But now, the more he thought about it, the more curious he became, as though long-dormant truths were awakening in his mind.

Abruptly, Ludlow got up and walked out of the lounge. He entered his living quarters and went into the small storage room. His eyes drifted over the boxes on the shelves. There! On the top shelf was an old brown cardboard box. That looked like the one. Pulling the box off the shelf, Ludlow opened the lid. Books. They were his old seafaring manuals, the ones that had taught him so much about sailing. He lifted them out of the box. Underneath he found the prayer book that had been his father's. And then, there it was—his father's Bible.

Ludlow set the box down and took the black book in his hands. He opened the cover and stared at the signature: John Sidney Walker. He riffled the pages, noting that some of them were stuck together after years of lying unopened in the humidity of Belize.

Taking the Bible, Ludlow walked back out into the sunshine. He closed the Bible and smoothed the cover. He felt his breath coming in short, quick inhalations. Returning to the lounge, he resumed his seat in the chair. He gently opened the Bible on his lap and looked hopefully at the page.

> Have mercy upon me, O God, according to thy lovingkindness: according unto the multitude of thy tender mercies blot out my transgressions. (Psalm 51:1)

Something resonated in Ludlow's heart. He could have written those words. That was just what he was feeling. He wanted someone to pity him, to extend mercy to him, to feel what he was going through. He continued reading.

> Wash me throughly from mine iniquity, and cleanse me from my sin. For I acknowledge my transgressions: and my sin is ever before me. Against thee, thee only, have I sinned, and done this evil in thy sight: that thou mightest be justified when thou speakest, and be clear when thou judgest. (v. 2-4)

Eagerly, Ludlow read on. His mind was reeling. Had he sinned against God? Yes, he knew he had. He knew he was sinning. He felt the sin that contaminated his heart, but he also felt something drawing him to read on.

> Make me to hear joy and gladness; that the bones which thou hast broken may rejoice. Hide thy face from my sins, and blot out all mine iniquities. (v. 8, 9)

Yes, he certainly longed for joy and gladness. Ludlow felt tears swelling at the corners of his eyes. He desperately wanted to have a purpose, a reason for living. But what about his sin? Why did its ugliness have to intrude on this picture of gladness?

Like a drowning man gasping for air, Ludlow read on.

> The sacrifices of God are a broken spirit: a broken and a contrite
> heart, O God, thou wilt not despise. (v. 17)

A broken heart? He had that, all right. His heart felt shattered. His hopes were all lying in pieces around his feet.

"God, do you hear me?" Ludlow's first prayer was direct and simple. He waited, holding his breath; then he continued, "If you hear me, help me. No one came to the auction. No one came to buy and I am disgraced in front of all my friends. I have no family, no one to turn to. Do you care?"

His eyes were drawn back to the Bible. A verse from across the page caught his eye.

> The fool hath said in his heart, There is no God. (Psalm 53:1a)

He recalled his earlier image of God as someone distant and uninterested in people. He remembered thinking there probably was no God. Did that mean he was a fool? According to the Bible, it did. The realization hurt, although at the moment Ludlow certainly did feel like one—a complete, worthless fool.

"Okay, God, if you do care, if you do help people, please help me." Ludlow was amazed at how easy it was for him to talk to—well, yes, talk to God. "If you can help, then help me with my shame, my humiliation at failing to sell my motel."

He sat quietly for a moment and something told him the failed auction was not the real reason for his despair. There was something deeper going on. He was really crying out for God to meet some need much greater than a buyer for Mopan.

Once again he began reading the Bible. As though a dam had suddenly broken, torrents of tears poured down Ludlow's cheeks as he read Psalm after Psalm. He felt his nose begin to run and he had to continually wipe away his tears to clear his vision and continue reading. Ludlow Walker was crying like a baby . . . like a broken man. Hot tears chased each other down his cheeks and dripped onto the open pages of his father's Bible.

"Is that Mr. Walker, the owner?" one of the guests asked Teresa, staring at the weeping man.

"Yes," Teresa admitted with embarrassment, looking away from her boss.

"He is acting crazy," another woman spoke up.

"Mr. Walker, do you need a drink?" one of the men inquired as he walked over to where Ludlow was reading. "Are you sick?"

Ludlow lifted his reddened eyes briefly to the speaker's face. He shook his head decidedly and went back to reading the Bible. Two couples left the lounge, looking distinctly upset.

"He *is* crazy," one woman hissed to Teresa. "You had better call a doctor."

> Give ear to my prayer, O God; and hide not thyself from my sup-
> plication. Attend unto me, and hear me: I mourn in my complaint,
> and make a noise; (Psalm 55:1, 2)

This is absolutely bizarre, Ludlow thought. How in the world could the Bible know exactly what he was going through, sitting in his cocktail lounge, crying and reading? These were his words, the cry from his own heart.

A half-used packet of cigarettes was on the table beside him. The lighter lay next to them, ready for use. Suddenly Ludlow grabbed the cigarettes and the lighter. Standing up, he went to the bar. "Take these," he begged Teresa brokenly.

The startled girl drew back and stared at him.

"Take them, please. Throw them away."

Ludlow looked at the well-stocked bar behind the counter. He scanned the rows of bottles with distaste.

"The bar will close today," he said firmly, "and it will close for the last time."

The few people who were left in the lounge heard him. They fell silent and stared uneasily at him. There was no sound except the music, and even that stopped as Ludlow walked across the lounge and turned it off. A heavy silence filled the room. He walked back to his chair and picked up the Bible. For some reason, he felt better. He began to read again.

"Teresa, we will close at ten," Ludlow said firmly. "Only the people who want something to eat will be served. The bar is closed."

"You can't do that," Teresa protested. "The people will want to come in for their drinks until at least midnight."

Leaning forward over the bar, Ludlow said emphatically, "The lounge will close at ten." Then looking at her with new eyes, he said, "And you can sleep in one of the empty units tonight. We are through."

As the impact of his words hit home, Teresa began crying. "That lady was right. You are going crazy!" she screeched as she stormed out of the room.

A crushing burden filled Ludlow's heart. Oh, how he had sinned! How his sins had damaged not only himself, but also other people. With a fresh shower of tears, he thought of all the girls he had known and then disposed of as though they were not even humans. "Oh, God," he groaned brokenly, "how I have sinned."

He stumbled back to his chair. A customer came in, looked around, and then approached Ludlow.

"I want a martini," he demanded. "Where is the barmaid?"

Ludlow got up with his Bible in hand and walked around the back of the bar. Absentmindedly he served the customer, only lifting his eyes from the pages when he absolutely had to.

"You are reading the Bible?" The man was upset. "Why are you doing this? Everyone is saying you are going crazy, and I think they're right. You don't need to act so stupid just because no one showed up to buy your motel."

Ludlow waved him away without lifting his eyes from the Bible. The guest walked outside with his drink, shaking his head in disbelief.

The great stirring in Ludlow's heart made him only dimly aware of what was going on in his motel complex. He realized some people were leaving early and knew it must be because he was making them uncomfortable, but he didn't care. Whatever was happening inside him was so compelling that he simply could not care about his business. In fact, he longed for everyone to be gone. Ten o'clock just couldn't come quickly enough on this night.

"Is everyone in? Are all the guests inside the compound?" Ludlow asked Goff. "Please lock the gate if they are."

Teresa came out of Ludlow's house. "Shelly is not back yet. She left with Jeff. He said he needed to go somewhere to find a drink in good company." Her words were sharp and bitter.

Ludlow groaned. He couldn't lock up until everyone was in. Lifting his face toward the stars, he began praying, "God, can you bring Shelly back so I can go to bed? Will you do this for me, please?"

Would God hear him? Did He care enough to listen to a prayer from someone as sinful as Ludlow Walker?

"We were at the Fuchsia bar when all at once I felt the weirdest thing," Shelly told Teresa from her perch on the bed. "Suddenly I knew I had to come back—back here to Mopan."

"What do you mean?" Teresa was in no mood for more bizarre events. She was disgruntled at being turned out of Ludlow's house and having to share a room with her sister, even though she and Shelly had moved into this room together when they had first come to Mopan.

"I don't know what I mean," Shelly retorted defensively. "I just knew I had to get out of there."

"Was Jeff drunk?" Teresa asked, moving her suitcase to the floor.

"No. Well, not much. I don't know what it was. I just had to get out of there." Shelly's voice softened. "It was as though an angel or something was telling me to come back here."

Teresa snorted. "Don't talk about angels. You are not good enough to have any heavenly messengers speaking to you. Maybe black angels, though they are not angels. They're demons."

Shaking her head, Shelly said, "No, it was not that. I know how those spirits act. This was different. Anyway, I told Jeff I wanted to come back. He got mad, saying he was not coming back to this place where Mr. Walker had gone crazy and that he was going to stay and have a good time."

Teresa looked at her sister. "So?" she inquired finally.

"I was surprised at myself. The feeling that I needed to come back here was so strong that I told Jeff I was going to walk. So I left."

"But it is seven miles back here," Teresa said. "Are you going crazy too?"

Shelly shrugged. "I started walking away when Jeff pulled up beside me and told me to get in the car. All the way here he kept yelling at me for being stupid and crazy. When he let me out, he left in a hurry."

Teresa looked out the window. "Something strange is going on around here," she muttered. "Something really, really weird."

———

"You did it!" Ludlow was in bed, lying flat on his back, staring into the darkness. "God, you answered my prayer." His voice was soft, as though speaking too loudly might make something precious disappear.

"I can hardly believe it. You made Shelly come home so soon after I asked you to do it. You do hear my prayer. You do care for me." Tears pooled once more in the man's eyes, but this time, they were not bitter tears or even tears of repentance, but tears of joy as he felt the love of God flooding his heart. "You love me, God! Oh, you love me and I don't deserve it! Thank you, thank you!" Ludlow felt his heart swell with gratitude and awe.

———

"You are still here," Ludlow said in amazement, sitting up in bed. He looked at the bedside clock. Six o'clock. It was still dark outside, but the eastern sky was faintly glowing.

"God, you are still here. I can feel you!" Ludlow got up and looked in the mirror. His reflection stared jubilantly back at him. He was still strong and tall with no signs of aging on his face. But the man looking back at him in the mirror was different. Something profound had happened to him.

The wonderful feeling that had filled him the night before was still in his heart. He had slept the entire night, and now he felt so refreshed, so full of energy, he thought he might explode. No longer did he feel washed out, old, or devoid of motivation. Ludlow wanted to move. He had to move. He pulled on his sneakers. He would run! Run outside in the glorious morning!

The trail that encircled the seven acres of Mopan was a hiking trail the guests had often enjoyed. It was light enough for Ludlow to see the path as it led between the shrubs and tall grasses. He began to run.

Suddenly Ludlow could not contain himself any longer. Throwing up his arms, he began speaking out loud, "Thank you, God! I know you hear me! I know you care about me, even though I do not deserve your attention."

The morning was dawning as the exultant man ran down the trail. There was no earthly ear to hear, no one to marvel at what was happening inside this man who was usually so firmly in control of himself.

Now here he was, Ludlow Walker, forty-four years old, running down the Belizean trail while praising God at the top of his voice. His feet skimmed the hard-packed dirt, his arms at times pumping madly as he ran, at other times lifted toward heaven as tears of joy streamed down his cheeks. Ludlow felt a fountain of words well up from deep inside his inner being.

"It's heart language, God," he panted, stopping to catch his breath. "It's language that you must have put inside me. Oh, thank you for this wonderful time with you."

Mondays at Mopan were almost always slow as the guests departed and quietness settled over the compound. Ludlow went back to his house so full of joy that he was not even hungry.

"Call Miss Nancy." The voice of the Spirit was speaking to him again.

Miss Nancy from the Mennonite mission in Hattieville. Why was he to call her? A vision of the white woman's smiling face floated into his memory. Miss Nancy with the wide smile. Never before had he really understood that smile. It had just belonged to the American woman who had been in Belize for years helping people, selling chickens, and visiting the poor and elderly. But always she had that smile.

Was she . . . did she have what God had given to him? Ludlow laughed out loud. He went to the telephone. Even as he heard the ring at the other end, Ludlow felt sure that, yes, Miss Nancy would know what had happened to him. The same thing must have happened at one time to her.

"I'm sorry, she is not here. She won't be back until tomorrow." The voice at the other end was courteous, but not the voice that Ludlow wanted to hear.

"This is Ludlow Walker. I really need to talk to Miss Nancy. I will call again."

"Okay." The telephone fell silent. Who else could he call? Was there anyone else who would understand what had happened, what was happening to him?

He called no one else. God had told him to call Miss Nancy, so he would wait. Today, he would talk with God some more and just enjoy His presence again. Ludlow reached for his Bible.

NEW LIFE

"Now I look back and I am not sure just when it happened," Ludlow said earnestly, looking at the two women. "But sometime on that Sunday afternoon, something changed in my heart. Right in here." Ludlow placed his big hand over his chest. "It was something so powerful that it lasted all through the night, all day yesterday, and today it is still there!" His voice was tinged with wonder as he shook his head slowly, trying to grasp the reality of this new experience. "The presence of God is still here!"

The two women seated on the outdoor patio at Mopan were listening intently. Miss Nancy had brought her friend, Alta, when she had come in response to Ludlow's telephone call that morning.

"I suddenly lost all my desire for wealth and prestige," Ludlow told them. "I find myself now only wanting to experience the presence of God in my life. For some reason I feel so deeply loved by God." Tears rolled down his cheeks as he shared what was happening to him.

"Oh, Mr. Walker, we are so happy for you!" Miss Nancy said radiantly.

"Do you think I am crazy? I know the employees here think I have lost my mind. The guests are all spreading the word that Mr. Walker has gone crazy. I am getting telephone calls from my business associates and prominent people in the government, asking me if I am all right. I know why they are calling. They have heard that I've lost my mind."

"You are not going crazy. On the contrary, you are finally in your right mind," Miss Nancy said seriously. "When God does a work in our hearts, He makes everything new. Your heart is made new. You have been born again."

"That's it," Ludlow replied eagerly. "I feel like I have a new heart. You call that being born again? That is a good term—born again. I sure feel like I've been born as a new person."

"It's not our term. The Bible refers to that experience as the new birth," Alta said quietly.

"It does? I want to read it," Ludlow said eagerly. "I've been reading in the Psalms and so many times I felt as though the words in the Bible were my words, my thoughts, and my feelings exactly."

"That is the Spirit of God making a connection to what is going on in your spirit," Miss Nancy told him. "When God changes us, we have new eyes, new understanding, and most importantly, a new nature. God takes our stony, fleshly heart out of our lives and gives us a new heart."

Ludlow lifted his eyes toward the blue sky and a broad smile spread over his face. "Thank you, Lord! I thank you for coming to give me a new heart."

There was a moment of silence before Ludlow said slowly, "You know, when people started telling me I was crazy and had lost my mind, I did wonder sometimes if that was the case. I feel so different, all washed and clean inside, and the things I used to want to do don't even appeal to me anymore. So it is good to know that I am not going crazy, but that I am coming into my right mind." With a chuckle he added, "Actually, if this is going crazy, I don't think I mind." They all laughed together.

"Would you like the pastors from the Mennonite mission to come and visit with you?" Miss Nancy asked. "I am sure you have many more questions, and I know they would be happy to meet with you and pray for you."

"Oh, yes!" Ludlow replied eagerly. "It is so wonderful to talk with people who know what I am experiencing. By all means tell the pastors they are welcome."

Ludlow felt his heart would burst with joy as he listened to Miss Nancy pray for him. Her words were so direct, so simple, merely asking God to bless and direct this new child born of the Spirit. But most of all, her prayer was that he would always know the presence of Jesus in his life.

"Amen!" Ludlow's voice rang out loud and triumphant. "Thank you so much for coming! You ladies are angels—angels of encouragement."

"It is Jesus who has made it possible for God to come and give you a new heart," Hughdelle Ysaguirre told Ludlow. "When Jesus came and lived on earth, died on the cross, and rose again from the grave, He released a power by His Spirit that comes into the hearts of all who believe and cry out for help."

"Jesus," Ludlow said softly. "Thank you, Jesus."

The three men who had come the next day had greeted him warmly. Besides Hughdelle, there was Gilbert Stevens and an American brother, Robert Yoder.

"I'm convinced it is real," Miss Nancy had told them joyfully. "When I first got the phone call from Mr. Walker, I was skeptical because I only remembered him as an ungodly man from Mopan. I made sure I took Alta along, and I didn't even go inside that motel, because I know the kind of reputation the place has. But as he told us his testimony, both Alta and I felt sure that God had come and changed this man's life. Please go and visit him. He doesn't even seem to understand who Jesus is, but he is just longing to know more, and I can tell he loves God with all his heart."

The three men had not been with Ludlow very long before they realized that what Miss Nancy had told them was true. Wisely, they opened their Bibles and showed Ludlow that Jesus, God's own Son, had made it possible for us to experience life in Him.

"The Holy Spirit? That's who lives inside my heart?" Ludlow was excited. "That was the Spirit of God that I felt the morning I was running along the trail? That was His language I heard? Wonderful!"

A murmur of assent came from the three men.

"When God comes into someone's heart, He not only lets us know by acknowledging the fact, but also by giving us a witness of that new birth by filling us with His Spirit. That is what you felt," Gilbert said. "I remember well when that happened to me."

"It still is happening," Ludlow said reverently. "There are times when I am reading the Bible, or praying, or just thinking about what has happened, and suddenly I feel something stir inside me. So that is the Holy Spirit." He took a deep breath and once more placed his hand over his heart.

Ludlow had many questions for his visitors. He wanted to know more about this new life. Like a young child, he eagerly absorbed all that the men told him.

"Yes, I know what you are saying is true. I can feel it inside," Ludlow kept saying as he nodded his head.

"You are welcome to come join us at church," Hughdelle told him. "We worship God and we pray together in our services. We have teaching and encouragement for the believers and we preach the Gospel to the unsaved."

"Unsaved. That is a good word," Ludlow told him. "That describes me when I was still all caught up with my own world." His eyes wandered thoughtfully around the compound and he sighed, "There is so much to learn. I look at my business here and I don't know what I am to do with it. Something tells me it is wrong to run this kind of business."

Robert spoke up gently, "The Holy Spirit will guide you, Mr. Walker. Do not try to figure it all out immediately. Just walk by faith, one step at a time and let God give you wisdom."

The other two men nodded their agreement.

The unmistakable anointing of God's Spirit was upon the little group as his new friends encouraged Ludlow and prayed with him, their spirits uniting as children of God.

"We have a prayer meeting on Wednesday," Hughdelle told Ludlow. "Why don't you come and tell our people what God has done and is doing in your life?" He reached out and hugged Ludlow warmly in parting.

For just a moment, Ludlow felt awkward, for he had never been hugged like this before. Then something broke inside him and he hugged Hughdelle and the other two men with enthusiasm. This was good! This love was of God.

"When you surrender your life to God, you must be willing to come to Him just as you are. Don't think you can clean up your life or improve your behavior or do anything else to make Jesus accept you. You can come just as you are, admit your sinful condition, repent, and Jesus will make all things new in your life."

Ludlow sat spellbound, listening to the speaker at the Mennonite church. He had never seen this man before, but it did not matter. This man was speaking truth, a truth that resonated deep inside his heart.

"The reason we call it the Gospel is because it is the Good News, the news that Jesus came to earth to save sinners.

"When we surrender our lives to the control of Jesus, something remarkable happens. We get power from God through the Holy Spirit and are transformed into a new person." Sanford Yoder paused and looked out over the congregation.

The crowd consisted mostly of Belizeans, but the mission workers from the States were there too. Ludlow looked around him. He saw a number of people listening intently and nodding their heads in agreement. A few others looked unhappy, but he could tell that the truth of the message was making an impact on everyone.

"One of the most important things we can do after we have made a commitment to follow Jesus is to tell other people. When we speak of that which God has done in our hearts, it strengthens us. There are times when the spoken word then makes an impact on other people's lives and they, too, want to know and experience the new birth."

That was something Ludlow understood. Within him something powerful was building up. He wanted to tell people about the wonderful thing that was happening to him. In fact, he had already spoken to Teresa when she had told him on Monday morning that she was leaving Mopan.

"Teresa, I know you think I am crazy, but something wonderful has happened to me. God has showed me how much He loves me, and I want to live for Him the rest of my life." It had been a new experience to speak like this, but Ludlow spoke from his heart. "I am truly sorry for the way I have treated you. I know it was selfish and wrong of me," he had continued simply.

With a toss of her head, Teresa had merely said, "I know that too."

Now, sitting in church, Ludlow painfully remembered all the women he had used in his life. With a pang, he thought of Millicent. In spite of the joy he found in his salvation, a huge feeling of remorse rose up in him as he thought of his wife and children. "Oh, God, give me back my family," he murmured brokenly.

"We have here with us this evening someone who recently experienced the change I have been talking about," Sanford was saying. "There is always great joy in our hearts to hear of someone who has become a child of God. Now we are going to hear about God's marvelous work in the life of Ludlow Walker."

Ludlow stood and faced the congregation. He swallowed nervously several times and then began to speak.

"Many of you know of me," he began humbly. "You know me as the owner of Mopan Motel and probably thought I was a happy, successful businessman. But I want to tell you that even though from the outside I looked happy and successful, I was not. I was looking for the wrong things and thought that money and position could meet my needs."

All eyes were fixed on the tall man as he spoke. Indeed, many of them had known him by name or had seen his pictures in the newspapers.

"My life started falling apart after my wife and children moved to Florida," Ludlow said with emotion. "I tried to distract myself with even more business ventures and hoped to fill the empty space in my heart with wrong things."

Lifting his head, Ludlow continued simply, "God came to me. In my cocktail lounge at Mopan, I began reading my father's Bible, and suddenly I started to cry. I felt things happening inside that I had never felt before. I heard God speak to me.

"I was losing my desire for the things I used to enjoy. I was longing instead to have real joy and peace in my life. And God came! Suddenly I felt the love of God just come over me! Something incredible was happening in my heart!" Ludlow was crying unashamedly now and many of his listeners were wiping their eyes as well.

"The next morning I got up and God was still there. I went outside and began running on the hiking trail, and I felt words of praise and love come up out of my heart. There I was, praising God and feeling His love for me! I didn't even know until later that it was Jesus who did all this for me and that He sent His Holy Spirit to move into people who wanted God. I only knew that God loved me very deeply, and I was so sorry for my life, for all my sins."

The silence was broken only by Ludlow's heavy breathing. "I love the Lord Jesus Christ with all my heart, and I am learning to listen to the voice of God and to obey." He started to sit down but then stood again. "Please pray for me. Pray that I could get my family back again," he implored. Burying his head in his hands, Ludlow wept. All around him people were weeping also.

"Brother Ludlow," Miss Nancy said after the meeting, "I will be praying for you. I will pray that God restores your wife and children to you. You are not alone. We as God's children will band together and pray faithfully for this. There's a verse from Proverbs that I want you to claim: 'Trust in the Lord with all your heart.' God cares very deeply for you and wants your family together again."

Ludlow looked at his new friend. "You called me Brother Ludlow?" he asked wonderingly.

Miss Nancy smiled, "Why, yes. You are my brother now. All of God's children are brothers and sisters in the Lord."

"Brother Ludlow. I like that better than Mr. Walker. It makes me feel like a part of God's family," Ludlow said with satisfaction.

"Thank you for sharing your testimony with us tonight." Many of the people in the congregation wanted to meet Ludlow and shake his hand. "How wonderful it was to hear what God did for you. We loved having you here and we welcome you back anytime."

Ludlow simply nodded his head in silent amazement. He had never dreamed that so many strangers would immediately become his friends. It was like getting an instant family!

"Thank you, God! Thank you for making me your son." In the loneliness of his bedroom Ludlow could pray aloud to God. "Thank you for letting me know how much you care for me. I feel your love and care through your people. These people are showing me who you are because of how they love me and each other."

Ludlow did not yet know of the verse in John 13:35 where Jesus said, "By this shall all men know that ye are my disciples, if ye have love one to another," but he knew it because he personally was experiencing it.

CHAPTER 15

OUT WITH THE OLD

"You can have that window for ten dollars," Ludlow told the Belizean man. "I have more than twenty of them if you want that many."

"Yes, sir!" The man tried to hide his excitement. "These are mighty fine windows."

Ludlow nodded absentmindedly. He heard another truck approaching Mopan and watched as two men dismounted from the cab.

"Is this the place where building supplies are being sold?" the driver asked questioningly, looking around the compound. "I think this is the address I was given."

"This is the place," Ludlow assured him. "Doors, windows, stoves, cooking utensils, towels, sheets . . . everything is for sale."

"You are getting ready to build again? Build bigger?"

Shaking his head and smiling slightly, Ludlow said, "No, I am tearing down this motel. I will not be building here again. I want this place destroyed."

For a second the two men looked at Ludlow as if dazed. They watched as buyers walked among the stacks of windows and doors, inspecting the merchandise. Without saying anything further, they joined the milling crowd.

"Thank you, Jesus," Ludlow breathed, watching the activity. It was working. The plan God gave him was working.

"Tear it down." Those were the words Ludlow had heard during his early morning prayer on the hiking trail. He had not protested for even a moment. So great was his desire to do whatever God told him to do, so thankful was he for his salvation through Jesus, so eager was he to show his gratitude, that Ludlow had immediately made plans to destroy Mopan.

"You could sell at a reduced price and still make money. Mr. Walker, you will regret what you are doing. When you come to your senses, you'll be sorry." The protests came from his former business associates, from people like Ben Feinstein who had seen his advertisements and heard that Mopan was being torn down.

"I am doing what God is telling me to do. I am learning to listen to God's voice," Ludlow had told them all calmly but firmly.

"Do you think it is good stewardship to sell your assets at bargain prices when there are so many places where you could donate the proceeds from the sale of Mopan? Why don't you ask God to send a buyer for the motel in its present condition?" The questions from people who claimed to be Christians were harder to answer. They sounded more reasonable. More tempting.

"If God has spoken to you, listen to His voice," his friends at the Mennonite church told him. "Do not listen to well-meaning people who don't know your situation."

"If I sell Mopan as it is, someone else will continue the business like I used to run it. There will be drunken orgies and all kinds of ungodly practices going on there. No, the only way I know to stop it is by tearing it down. I don't want my sins to be taken on by anyone else," Ludlow declared with tears. "I know I have been instrumental in ruining marriages, supporting addictions, and providing a place for immoral people to contact each other. In the name of Jesus, I want all that to stop. I ruined my marriage in this place and I cannot go on this way."

With support from the church, Ludlow had begun to advertise, "Giveaway prices. Liquidation sale. Everything must go." At first it was as though people could not believe it was true. They had been hearing about some strange happenings at Mopan, but when the advertisements appeared in the newspapers and on handbills in town, only a few had responded. When those early buyers had returned with their purchases and the news that it really was true, people began flocking to Mopan to snatch up the bargains.

"Start at that end and take out everything that can be sold," Ludlow had told the contractor he hired to demolish his motel. "Just stack it in piles and I will price the items later."

Leaving only his living quarters and a few other rooms intact, Ludlow watched calmly as the demolition took place. Daily he watched with satisfaction as the vestiges of his old life crumbled into rubble. He experienced no regrets. Ludlow's joy and fellowship with God were too real, too precious for him to regret his radical obedience.

———————————

"We have reservations for four." The young man's voice was loud and demanding. "We expected a decent motel when we made reservations, not this dump. It looks like a hurricane hit you. Do you still have rooms?"

Ludlow nodded and looked past the man at the passengers getting out of the car. There was another man and two girls. They were talking loudly and Ludlow saw with dismay the dark brown bottles they were holding.

"You are welcome to cancel if you like," he said courteously. "I tried to let you know I am closing Mopan, but I could not get an answer on the phone."

"Of course not. We've been on the road for three weeks since we left Atlanta," the guest retorted irritably. "We want a room."

Ludlow had saved the four rooms on the other side of his living quarters, and those people whom he had not been able to contact to cancel their reservations were still using those units. "Let me take down your information," Ludlow requested. He took a pen and copied the names and addresses of the guests.

"Where is the owner?" demanded the driver.

"I am the owner," Ludlow said calmly, taking down the information from the passport.

There was a snort of disgust from the man. "Another Martin Luther King, huh? You black people think you can do anything you like. Well, we'll show you yet."

Ludlow said nothing. Obviously, these people were not sympathetic to the civil rights movement that was sweeping the southern United States.

"King got what he deserved," the man said acidly.

Ludlow knew he was being baited. He said nothing, but continued to write.

"We had already heard you were tearing down your motel," the young man said, leaning over the counter. His tone was far from friendly.

"Is that right?" Ludlow replied mildly, continuing to write.

"In Belize City, they say you are ruining this part of the country with your foolishness."

Ludlow looked up quickly. Why did he feel a finger of fear run up his spine?

Outside, the other three were talking loudly, gesturing toward the demolished part of Mopan.

"They say you are going crazy," the cold voice continued. "You know, you blacks think you can just do whatever you want. March in the cities, demand equal rights for all your people, build motels and demolish them without a thought of what that does to our plans. We came here expecting to see a fully functioning motel and bar. Now we find half the place torn down. The bar looks deserted. I haven't seen anyone around except you."

"I have dismissed all the workers. I am closing the motel. If you like, I will refund your deposit and you can find another place to stay. The Flamingo Hotel is only thirteen miles from here, and I can call and see if they have any rooms." Ludlow looked straight at the young man.

"Ben, what is going on in here?" The other man's voice came from the doorway. "Do we get a room in this dump or not?"

Ben turned to face his companion. "Sam, this guy is the owner and he says we can have a room. The bar is closed and he is the only one here. He says we can try the Flamingo if we don't want to stay here."

A look that Ludlow did not like passed between the two men.

Sam swayed slightly on his feet and then looked at the girls outside. "Let's take the rooms. I don't want to go to some other place in this hot country. It is even hotter here than in Georgia."

"You guys from Chicago think anything over eighty degrees is hot," his companion retorted. Turning to Ludlow he demanded, "Give me the keys."

"And get us something to drink. We will come out to the patio after we dump our stuff," Sam ordered.

It was getting dark before the guests appeared for their drinks. Ludlow served them soft drinks. He had determined never again to serve alcohol to any guests. Obviously, these guests did not need strong drinks from the bar. They had brought their own.

"Heard you don't serve liquor anymore," Sam said, sloshing his soda on the table.

"No, sir, I don't. I know God does not want me to serve intoxicating drinks anymore," Ludlow told them.

"Stupid ideals," Sam snorted. The girls giggled nervously.

Ben leaned forward and glared at Ludlow. His eyes gleamed menacingly in the dusk. "You know what happened to Martin Luther King and all his religious ideas, don't you?" He slowly slid his forefinger across his own throat and looked meaningfully at Ludlow.

Another stab of fear went up Ludlow's spine.

"If you continue your crazy actions, you will end up the same way," Ben said icily.

The wind that tossed the palm trees swept over the outside table where the four were sitting. Ludlow was used to the coastal storms sweeping in from the sea. The breezes were always welcome, but the winds were often the beginnings of tropical thunderstorms.

But his mind was not on the weather at the moment. He thought of the collection of firearms in his house. He was the only one left on the staff at Mopan. What were these people up to?

"Jesus," he breathed softly to himself.

The girls clutched at their clothes as the wind increased. When the first drops of rain fell, the four scurried off to their rooms. Ludlow got up and walked into the courtyard, looking up at the sky. He glanced at the rooms where the guests were staying. Uneasy thoughts crept into his mind. Had someone sent them to harm him? He realized he had made enemies by some of his drastic actions.

Once more he thought of his guns, but the voice of the Spirit in his heart made it clear that this was not a time to trust in weapons. Normally, Ludlow would not have been afraid. But in this case, there was something sinister, even demonic, that threatened to devastate him with fear. A strong, muscular man, Ludlow had always prided himself in his own strength and had never backed away from any antagonist. But this was different. The whole battle between good and evil seemed to be playing itself out at Mopan.

"Jesus, help me," Ludlow prayed out loud, lifting his face up to the rain. "I feel evil all around me."

Martin Luther King. Murdered. Was that going to happen to him? Were these drunken men sent to kill him?

"Lord, I am ready for death. I know that will simply mean I will be able to see you face to face and behold your glory with new eyes. I am ready to come to you if this is my time."

Without warning, a bolt of lightning flashed out of the sky and struck a mere thirty feet from where he stood, sending a ball of fire across the courtyard. The clap of thunder that followed shook the ground powerfully. With a leap, Ludlow set off running through the rain, out the gate and down the road, his long legs racing away from the lightning strike.

"Why are you running? You said you were ready to die." God's Spirit arrested Ludlow in midflight. He stopped and, with a sob, knelt right down on the road.

"Oh, Lord," he prayed, rain streaming down over his drenched face and clothes, "I'm sorry. I'm sorry for not trusting in you. I don't need to be afraid. You are stronger than any evil force anywhere. I do trust in you." As the fear left, a wonderful warm feeling of trust and comfort flooded his heart.

Leaping to his feet, Ludlow flung his arms upward and began laughing, the rain washing his face. "Thank you, God! Thank you for sending the lightning and thunder. This is your voice. This is your might demonstrating what you can do. Your power is real!"

Turning, he ran back to Mopan. Exultantly he knocked on the guest room door. "Come out!" he challenged fearlessly. "Come see what my

God can do! See the mighty power of my Lord!" His triumphant laugh rang out in the night as the wind whipped sheets of rain against the windows of the guest room.

A curtain was pulled away for an instant and a face peered out. Ludlow knew he must look ridiculous, dancing and praising God in the middle of the storm, but he didn't care. Now let the cowering guests see the demonstration of his God. Yes, God was in control!

"Timmy, take these bottles of Jack Daniels and use them to kill the grass along the sidewalks," Ludlow instructed the maintenance boy early the next morning.

"Yes, sir," Timmy replied with an indulgent smile. Killing grass with whiskey? That was a new one, but if the boss man said so, why, he would do exactly that. Ludlow had earlier gathered up all the open bottles from the bar and had carried them outside into the storm-washed morning.

"Here are some more when those are gone," Ludlow said, waving at the bottles.

Timmy did as he had been instructed. He poured the whiskey carefully along the sidewalks, and as some splashed onto the warm concrete, the vapors rose and the smell of alcohol was heavy in the morning air.

Ben opened the door of the guest room but stopped in his tracks when he saw the spectacle outside. "What are you doing?" he asked in astonishment as he saw the expensive liquors being poured onto the grass.

"Oh, just using weed killer," Ludlow laughed. "I don't know of a better use for this stuff. Do you?"

Ben disappeared briefly; then Sam's face joined him at the door as they watched the bottles being emptied. Ludlow had gone back into the bar, and loading the wheelbarrow with bottles, he called to Timmy, "When you get done, dig a hole behind the little shop. We are going to be breaking a lot of full bottles and burying the glass."

The guest room door shut hastily, and only minutes later there was a hurried exit as the four guests piled into their car. Without a word or even a wave, they sped out of the compound and disappeared down the road.

Ludlow lifted one hand toward the sky as he declared, "Lord Jesus, this day I mark an end to Mopan. As a memorial, we will smash all the bottles that are left. I don't care how much they are worth. This is my testimony that I will trust you the rest of my life!" With a joyful laugh, he pushed the wheelbarrow toward the area behind the shop where Timmy was already digging industriously.

16

REPAIRING THE DAMAGE

Dear Millicent,

I must tell you about an amazing thing that happened to me. I will try to explain in this letter what God has done in my life.

I tried to sell Mopan in order to buy that land along the ocean and build a better hotel. No one bid on Mopan at the auction. I was bitterly disappointed, and all at once I realized that my life was worth nothing. I did not have anything of lasting value to sustain my hopes any longer.

As I sat in the cocktail lounge, I was thinking about life and how I was being ruined. First of all my family was ruined and now my business venture was ruined. For some reason, I remembered the Holy Bible. I began to think about some things I had learned in school. I wanted to read the Bible and remembered my father's Bible. I did not know where it was at first, but I found it in the storage room on the top shelf. I took it and returned to my chair. I opened it to Psalm 51 and began reading.

Millicent, please find a Bible and read what I read that day. I knew it was my prayer and that I indeed had sinned. I kept on reading, and hardly even knowing it, I began to cry. I cried and read and cried and read some more. All afternoon I read the Bible. I closed the cocktail lounge at ten o'clock and went to my room. I prayed and cried myself to sleep.

The next morning I felt full of energy and went on the jogging trail. I found myself talking to God. The more I prayed, the greater the joy inside me grew. My heart began to overflow and I don't know what all I said, but it was all to God.

I sent for Miss Nancy, (you remember the Mennonite lady I used to get our chickens from?) and she and another girl came. I told them what had happened. They were so glad for me and told me that God was coming into my heart.

I did not know what all that meant, but I was so filled with joy and relieved to find someone who understood what was happening inside me. Everyone around here thought I was going crazy.

I started going to the Mennonite church, and they are teaching me a lot about Jesus and the Christian life. They are becoming my good friends.

Well, I soon saw that having the motel and the cocktail lounge was part of what had destroyed our marriage, and so I began to demolish the motel. I poured out the open bottles of whiskey and broke the full bottles. Timmy helped me bury them behind the shed.

Millicent, I have repented of my selfishness and of my sins and God has forgiven me. Now I am writing to you and asking you and the children to forgive me as well. I am sorry for the thoughtless and inconsiderate husband I have been. I see now how I neglected you and overworked you. I did not treat you as a husband should treat his wife. I was way too busy and involved with my business life to truly be what I should have been.

Also, I am sorry for how I treated Dawn and was not a true father to her. As for little Junior, I was mostly glad to have him as a son to help my position. I am truly sorry for this.

Millicent, I still love you. I miss you and the children now more than ever, and I pray to God that someday we can all be together as a family again.

> *Please forgive me.*
>
> *Ludlow*

Millicent folded the letter and stood up to look out the window. The Florida traffic swirled busily down the street outside the apartment building. Staring with unseeing eyes, Millicent tried to think clearly. Was this just another way to get her to come back to him in Belize? Did

Ludlow want her to think that he was having mental problems and that she needed to come back to help him?

Picking up the letter, she read parts of it again. She was baffled by all this talk about God and Jesus. She had never even heard Ludlow mention God. If someone asked him about his religion, he always said he didn't really believe God was interested in his life. Now it was God this and Jesus that.

Reading his father's Bible? She thought he had clung to it only because it had belonged to his deceased father. Why would he suddenly take an interest in that? It was puzzling. Millicent thought about his other letters, written after he had realized that she and the children were making their home in Florida. Those messages had been demanding and commanding, never pleading. After she had sent the papers notifying him of the divorce, his letters had become bitter and accusing. Finally she had stopped opening mail from Ludlow.

Then, for a long time, there had been no word from him. No news, nothing. Now, all at once, this long letter that made no sense. Well, it made some sense, but it was certainly not written by the Ludlow she knew. This man was different; he was someone she had not even known existed. With a sigh, Millicent prepared to leave for her job. She was glad to get out of the apartment, away from that strange letter.

"They said you had gone crazy." Ivy Walker sat in the living room chair in Ludlow's house and rested her hands in her lap. " 'Completely crazy,' they said."

Ludlow smiled at his aged mother. It was so good to see her again. Traveling to Belize at her age must have been difficult, but she had been concerned enough by the reports that reached her to make the trip.

"I imagine," Ludlow said reflectively. "Yes, I can imagine that most of my former associates and acquaintances really did think, or still think, that I have gone crazy." With a chuckle, he said, "Come to think of it, if someone else would have done the things I have done these last two months, I would have questioned his sanity as well. Pouring out the expensive whiskies, tearing down the motel, and selling land at give-away prices must all look like the actions of a madman." Then reaching out and taking his mother's hand lovingly in his own, he asked, "Mother, what do you think?"

Ivy looked deeply into her son's eyes. She studied the smile on his face. "From what you have told me, son, I think now you are in your right mind," she stated confidently.

Squeezing her hand, Ludlow said simply, "Thank you, Mother."

"I know you have found peace in your heart with God. I can see it in your eyes," his mother smiled.

"It is all because of Jesus. When God first touched my heart and I found myself weeping before Him, I knew almost nothing about Jesus. At the Mennonite church, they are teaching me about Jesus Christ, the Son of God. It is He who has made it possible for God to come and live inside us in the form of the Holy Spirit. We are saved by Jesus."

Ivy nodded. "I am so glad you have found your peace."

Ludlow bowed his head and prayed silently. How much did his mother understand? Was she still thinking of God as he himself had done in his youth? Did she picture an unapproachable God as he remembered from the stiff, formal church setting in Jamaica?

"Jesus is so alive," Ludlow exclaimed passionately. "He lives in me and by His Spirit I can have fellowship with Him. I can ask anything I want and wait on Him for answers. He has filled me with His Spirit."

"And Millicent?" his mother inquired. "What does she say about all this?"

Ludlow felt the familiar pain that gripped his heart whenever he thought of his wife and children. He sighed and said slowly, "I wrote a letter to her, telling her what happened, but I haven't received a response. I am praying that she can forgive me for all the wrongs I have done to her."

"Jesus said, 'I am the way, the truth, and the life: no man cometh unto the Father, but by me.' " The white man standing in front of the little congregation in Belize read the words distinctly. "There is only one way to heaven and that is through Jesus. He wants us to repent from our sins, believe in the death and resurrection of Jesus Christ, and be saved."

Dawn Walker shifted on the bench beside the other girls her age and wondered briefly what had made her come back to Belize.

"Daddy wants you to come to a youth meeting they are having in Belize," her mother had told her. "He said he would pay your tickets."

"Why would I go?" Dawn frowned. "I haven't even seen Daddy for four years. I was twelve when we left Belize."

Her mother had not tried to persuade her to go. "It's up to you. Your dad has changed, that is one thing sure, but I will leave the decision up to you."

In spite of her initial decision not to accept her father's invitation, Dawn had suddenly given in and flown to Belize City. Her father had met her and taken her to what was left of Mopan—just his living quarters.

At first it had been rather strange to see the place where she had spent most of her childhood. Eventually she had found some old school friends and found it easy to speak Creole with them again.

But church? That was a different story. There was so much talk about Jesus.

The next speaker was a Belizean. He was darker than her father, and even though he spoke good English, he also sprinkled Creole words into his sermon.

"There is that longing inside every person that can only be filled with the presence of Jesus," Hughdelle addressed the young people. "Many people have tried to fill it with other things, like riches, pleasures, and addictive drugs, but nothing will satisfy it like the love of Jesus in your heart."

Dawn shifted her gaze to the people around her. Sprinkled among the black Belizeans were the Mennonites from the United States. They looked strange here, their white skin either pale and colorless or red from the sun. Several of them had tanned skin; they must be the ones who had lived here for a longer period.

Miss Nancy was there. Ludlow had introduced Dawn to his friend.

"Welcome, Dawn," Miss Nancy had said, her warm smile enveloping the newcomer. "I am so glad you came."

Dawn sighed and wondered why she had come. Why had she returned to a country that she used to dream of escaping? What had brought her back here, by her own choice, no less?

She remembered looking out across the flat landscape around Mopan as a young child, watching the sunset. She remembered how she used to dream about escaping back to New York City and away from this strange place. It had been hard to go to school in Belize City. At first her parents had enrolled her in a Catholic school known for the excellent education it offered. But there had been that episode when one of the nuns had spanked her furiously and her parents had promptly enrolled her in another school.

The last several years in Belize had settled into a tolerable routine, but from the moment she had set foot in Florida, Dawn had tried to push away every trace of her life in Belize. Throwing herself into her new school, she had largely succeeded in making a new life among her new friends.

"There is that yearning inside of you, and that is the Holy Spirit calling you to give your life to the Lord and be saved," Hughdelle said in closing. "Listen to the voice of the Spirit and let Jesus wash away your sins."

Sins. Did she have any? Dawn knew there were times when she had not been the good girl she tried to convince everyone else she was. Lately even her mother was on this bent about Jesus. She had started going to church and tried every Sunday morning to take her children with her.

"I have so much homework," Dawn had complained, trying to persuade her mother to let her stay at home. But her mother was too wise. She would remind her daughter to get her homework done on Saturday. Reluctantly she had gone to church with her mother and Ludlow Junior.

Now she stood along with the others for the dismissal prayer. There was a rustle as they gathered into small groups for the prayer and discussion period.

"What needs do you want to share for prayer?" Grace, the Belizean woman, asked her group. Several girls requested prayer for a deeper walk with God. One asked the group to pray for her sick mother.

"Dawn, are you a Christian? Do you want us to pray for you?" Grace asked in her blunt but kindhearted way.

Dawn was ready. She had heard Grace ask other girls the same question. "Oh, yes, I go to church," she said flippantly, trying not to think of the many times she tried to get out of attending.

For a moment Grace said nothing. Then turning to face Dawn, she said matter-of-factly, "I don't think you are."

"Excuse me?" Dawn drew her slim self indignantly upright in her chair. But Grace wasn't listening. She was already praying.

Dawn felt hot. What in the world was going on? That Grace! Shaming her in front of the other girls! Why, of course she was a Christian! She wasn't Muslim, was she?

"Speak clearly to all of us, Lord Jesus. Remove any doubt, any unbelief, and help us to be honest before you. Lord, help all these girls . . ." Dawn refused to listen any longer. She wanted to get away from these people. Suddenly she felt hemmed in, cornered, and imprisoned. Opening her eyes, she saw the other groups of people in prayer. Over by the door her daddy was praying with a group of boys.

What had happened to her life? What had happened to her daddy? And her mother? Why all this talk about being saved and Jesus and things like that? What did that have to do with her? Snatches of the sermon flitted through her memory. "Give your heart to Jesus. Repent, and be saved."

The rest of the afternoon Dawn tried to visit with the other girls, but something was different. Two more days, and then she could board the plane to go back to Florida. Back where, for the most part, life was the same and she did not have to think so much about her soul and about Jesus and about religion. She was intensely relieved when she could return with Daddy to his house.

"No, thanks," she replied with a strained smile when her father asked if she wanted to sit with him in the living room for a while. She saw the hurt in his eyes, but she closed the door to her room and collapsed on her bed, staring straight up at the ceiling. She felt she would go crazy just lying here and thinking. She found her small radio, put on her headphones, and pushed the button.

The journey is long and the road uphill and down.
The days and months and years take their toll.
Disappointments and delusions, strife and confusion
Come in big waves and threaten to drown you.

The singer paused while the music continued to play. Then the lyrics resumed.

But don't you quit believin'
Never stop believin'
No matter what, you cannot stop.
If you stop believin' you're lost.

Dawn wanted to scream. Lost! There was that word again. With her mind only half on the song, Dawn thought about the other words she had heard. For instance, being saved. She assumed being saved meant long skirts, sober faces, no fun, and everyone looking at you strangely.

"Come to Jesus, He will save you," she found herself thinking. The words of a song they had been singing all week drowned out the song on the radio.

Jesus. He was loving. Everyone said He was. Something tugged at Dawn's heart.

"Don't stop believin'," the radio sang again.

"Believe on the Lord Jesus Christ, and thou shalt be saved." It was Hughdelle who had read that just that morning.

"Jesus, please help me!" Dawn's cry was a mere whisper, but the One who is waiting tenderly for the prayer of any sincere heart came and began ministering to the lonely girl in her room. "I do believe in you, Jesus. I will let you be in control of my life. Forgive me, Jesus, for my sins and come into my life." Dawn's prayer was simple, yet she meant it with all her heart.

As the Holy Spirit filled her being, she exclaimed, "I do believe! I believe in Jesus! In God! I am not lost anymore!" Dawn felt a surge of joy spill through her.

"Oh, my daughter, thank you so much for coming." Ludlow drew his daughter to his side as her flight was announced. "I pray that we can all be back together as a family someday. But I am most thankful just now to God for your salvation in Jesus. It fills my heart with joy to think that my precious daughter has received Jesus in the same place where her daddy became a new man. This has been a blessed time together."

It was hard for Dawn to leave her father. This new man was in some ways as she had remembered him, but in so many other ways he was completely new. But now she knew what had made him different: it was the same Jesus who had begun to renew her heart.

She waved goodbye through her tears, grabbed her purse tightly, and turned to board the plane.

CHAPTER 17

WALKING IN LIGHT

"Brother Ludlow, we are rejoicing with you in your salvation," Brother Lester Gingerich said kindly, his face showing the warmth in his heart. "I have heard of your changed heart and your new life in Jesus, and I will be honored to baptize you, first of all as a child of God, and also as a sign of acceptance into the church here in Hattieville."

Ludlow bowed his head, overcome by the welcome he had received in this little fellowship. "Brother Lester, I know I don't understand some things about the Mennonite way of life, but I am willing to learn," Ludlow had said sincerely. "I know one of the biggest helps to me in my Christian life has been the kind way you people have accepted me and encouraged me on my spiritual journey."

Ludlow's mind returned suddenly to the present as he heard Brother Hughdelle begin to speak. Ludlow could hear the heartfelt sincerity as his friend and brother said, "Ludlow, I have seen the change God has worked in your life, and I have thanked Him many times for His amazing power. In the past few years we have heard of your life here in Belize, and like the Apostle Paul before he was converted, you were serving your own interests. However, now we can all see that serving God is the most important thing in your life."

Ludlow felt tears spilling from his eyes. "Oh, yes, brothers. To serve God is by far the most important thing in my life," he agreed. Then he paused before continuing in a broken voice, "And to get my family back together again is probably the second most important thing for me. I pray every day that Millicent will forgive me and take me back."

The two ministers said nothing as they realized again the agony Ludlow was going through at the mention of his estranged wife. Their hearts went out to the grieving man.

"We will pray with you," Brother Lester said finally, laying a sympathetic hand on the broad shoulders of the man sitting in front of him. Hughdelle nodded. He closed his eyes and began to pray. A holy hush settled over the little group as they once more brought their prayers for reconciliation and healing before the throne of the Great Physician.

In the days that followed, whenever the church gathered, the members faithfully joined Ludlow in prayer for his wife and children. "We pray for you and your family every day," numerous brothers and sisters told Ludlow. "We will stand with you in faith until we see our prayers answered."

"I know you pray. I feel the prayers," Ludlow gratefully told them again and again. "Most days my faith is strong, but I must confess that sometimes in the night, when sleep is far from me, I look into the future and wonder if she will ever take me back. I have treated her so unfairly and without feeling so many times. Oh, Lord, forgive me!" It was evident to all that Ludlow had deeply repented and longed for the day when he could prove his love for his wife and children.

"You don't need them anymore."

Ludlow was alone in his simple living quarters. His Bible was open, but this time he was not reading. His mind was traveling back into his old life, and the Spirit had just brought to his mind the collection of three guns he had acquired over the past few years.

"My trust is in you, Lord," Ludlow said out loud. He remembered that the church had faithfully taught people not to put their trust in weapons, but to trust in God for protection. In spite of that, the guns had remained in Ludlow's possession. This was not the first time he had been reminded of his collection, but this time he felt the Spirit speak directly about the issue.

Leaning forward, Ludlow thought of the past again. He always knew that he did not really need three guns to protect himself and his family. Yet he always had at least one gun in his vehicle wherever he went in Belize. Even in the States he had felt safest when he carried a concealed weapon.

"Jesus teaches us to love our enemies" was the oft-repeated message that the pastors in their fellowship taught. "If we trust in guns or weapons, we are not walking by faith or in the complete power of the Lord."

Ludlow placed his Bible on the table and rose decisively. He walked to the cabinet where he kept his guns. Taking a key from his pocket, he unlocked the case and lifted a pistol from the shelf. He pointed the firearm toward the floor and fingered the trigger. He looked at the other guns. What killing power lay in those cold, steel weapons! Countless lives had already been snuffed out by guns like these. Something akin to revulsion seized him, and he shut the door abruptly, locking it firmly.

The next morning before doing anything else, Ludlow emptied his gun cabinet. He wrapped all the weapons in blankets and put them into his truck and headed for Belize City. Pulling up in front of a two-story concrete building with a flight of steps leading to the front door, Ludlow parked his truck. Taking his burden in his arms, he walked up the steps.

"Commissioner Gilman, please," Ludlow told the uniformed officer at the desk.

The man nodded respectfully at Ludlow and pressed a button. "Ludlow Walker is here to see you, sir" he said into a microphone. After listening for a reply, he nodded and responded, "Yes, sir." He stood and escorted his visitor deferentially to the closed door. A brass plate on the door informed all that here was the office of the Belize City police chief.

"Mr. Walker." Commissioner Gilman rose and looked quizzically at the wrapped burden in Ludlow's arms.

"May I?" Ludlow nodded toward a side table.

"Oh, yes," Gilman assured him. As Ludlow placed the guns on the table and unwrapped them, the police chief watched with widening eyes.

"I no longer need these weapons," Ludlow said finally, turning to face the chief.

"Mr. Walker," Commissioner Gilman said as he lifted his right hand in protest, "whatever is going on? What are you doing?"

"I am turning in all my weapons," Ludlow replied with a smile. "I don't want them to fall into the hands of people who might use them to harm or kill someone, so I thought this would be the right place to bring them. I want to turn them over to you, and if you could record the registration numbers and sign a paper stating that these weapons are now property of the Belize City Police Department, I would be most grateful."

Gilman walked over to the guns. He picked up a pistol and then laid it back down. "Do you have permits for all these guns?" he inquired.

Ludlow nodded and pulled them from his pocket. He handed the papers to Gilman.

The commissioner glanced at them briefly and then handed them back to Ludlow. He walked back to his desk and motioned for Ludlow to take a chair. Shuffling papers on his desk, he looked at Ludlow and asked, "What makes you do this, Mr. Walker? This has never happened before in my tenure."

Ludlow nodded his head. "I believe you, sir. But let me tell you why I am doing this." Humbly and sincerely, Ludlow shared his testimony with the police chief. He talked about his life of trying to climb the ladder of success and prosperity to the detriment of his family. He told Gilman about his conversion as he read his father's Bible, and about the power of Jesus Christ entering his heart and changing his entire life. "For six months I have been walking in this new life, and believe me, it has been the most satisfying and glorious time in my life. I still carry heartaches because of mistakes I made in my former life, but now I have Someone who carries them for me.

"These guns," Ludlow continued, waving his hands toward the weapons on the table, "are a part of my former life and I don't need them any more for protection. I have the living Lord Jesus Christ for my protection, and He is more trustworthy than any earthly weapon."

As Ludlow's amazing story unfolded, Gilman kept glancing in bewilderment from his visitor to the guns. When Ludlow finally paused, the commissioner said, "Mr. Walker, yours is indeed a very remarkable and interesting story. Unfortunately, there is no protocol on how to proceed with this unusual situation."

Ludlow waited respectfully. He found it almost amusing to see the dilemma that faced the officer. How could he report this strange incident?

"But why not sell . . ." Gilman's voice trailed away as he recalled what Ludlow had told him earlier. "I guess you would be afraid the wrong people would get possession of these guns," he answered his own question. Again he studied the papers on his desk.

"Sir, if you would just record the serial numbers of the guns and write a note verifying that you have received them from me and that they are no longer in my possession, that is all I am asking for," Ludlow said, trying to help.

"This is causing a problem for me," Gilman said, furrowing his brows. "If I have these guns in my possession, I will have to submit a report on how I came to have them."

Ludlow waited silently, but his decision was already made. He had no intentions of walking out of that building with those guns still in his possession.

"All right, Mr. Walker," Commissioner Gilman said finally, but with obvious reluctance. "I will give you the document you request." Taking a sheet of paper, he began to write. "This will cause me an untold amount of grief," he grumbled under his breath.

Ludlow read out the serial numbers so that Gilman could record them. When the chief had finished, he wordlessly extended the signed document to Ludlow. With a courteous smile and thanks, Ludlow exited the building with a grateful heart. His steps were lighter as he walked to the parked truck. "Lord, that's one more thing taken care of," he said aloud as he started the engine. "I don't know where all else you will take me, but I am willing to be taken."

"Lord, if you want me to return to the States to be closer to Millicent and the children, please speak plainly to me," Ludlow prayed one evening. "Weeks are going past and the letters I send are not being answered except for occasional little notes from Millicent. I feel so helpless here in Belize, so far away from my family. I have gotten rid of Mopan and what is here to keep me? I need an answer from you, Lord. I don't want to act in my own flesh, but only by the direction of your Word and Spirit."

On into the night the troubled man poured out his heart to God. He loved the church in Belize, and he knew that he would always be grateful for the way they had accepted him with open arms. He was beginning to realize and appreciate how in his early Christian life, they had allowed him time to learn about their prescribed way of life rather than forcing it on him. They had been willing to let the Spirit teach him the new life of walking in the light.

Finally, before the new day broke, Ludlow received his answer. There was no audible voice or even a specific verse in the Bible that God used to reveal His will. Rather, it was Ludlow's earnest longing for his family that confirmed God's leading in his heart. He knew there would be far more opportunities to be a blessing to them and prove the reality of his changed heart if he was closer to them. Ludlow felt the blessed peace of God settle over his heart as he made the decision.

"We bless you, brother," the pastors from the church told him. "We understand and we send you gladly, although your presence will be sorely missed here. You have been a great encouragement to all of us."

So it was with many tears and fond embraces that his spiritual family sent Ludlow to the States, assuring him that they would never forget him. "We look forward to hearing the news of your reconciliation with your family," they told him in confident faith.

"My church family," Ludlow told them brokenly with tears, "may God bless you richly for all you have done for me. You have prayed with me, encouraged me, and accepted me so readily into your lives. You will always be carried in my heart."

The flight to Miami gave Ludlow time to reflect on the many changes that had taken place since he had moved to Belize. He remembered with what excitement he had faced the challenges of building the motel and how he had foolishly wanted to build an even bigger and better place than Mopan. He recalled the downward spiral of his life after Millicent and the children left, how he had finally reached bottom, and how, in that desperation, he had cried out for help.

"Oh, Lord, you have been so good to hear my cry," Ludlow prayed as the airplane began its descent into the Miami airport. "Now restore me to my family. Please restore me to my family."

A large chapter of his life was ending. The next chapter was about to begin. How would it end? Would Millicent ever consider accepting him back again? Would he be able to prove to her that he had indeed been changed?

"Trust," he sensed the Lord telling him.

Ludlow nodded his head. "Yes, Lord. I will trust in you. If I try to prove anything in my own strength, I will fail. You have to do it all, Lord."

The wheels of the aircraft hit the runway and Ludlow was in Florida—alone. And yet not alone, for once more he felt the presence of God with him.

CHAPTER 18

LAYING FOUNDATIONS

"I have asked Brother Ludlow Walker to share his testimony with us tonight," William McGrath said, putting his arm around Ludlow's shoulders. "He has an amazing story of how the Lord spoke to him, and all that happened next is a testimony of what the power of God can do in the heart of anyone who is willing to be led by the Spirit."

Ludlow looked at William and smiled; then he turned to address the congregation. A sea of faces looked up at him. Ludlow swallowed and began to speak.

"My name is Ludlow Walker and I am originally from Jamaica. But the most wonderful part of who I am is that I am a new person in Jesus Christ."

Across the congregation, encouraging smiles were directed toward him. Taking a deep breath, Ludlow continued, "I am not used to speaking to large crowds, but when Brother McGrath asked if I would share my testimony in these tent meetings in Ohio, my first thought was, *Oh, I get to tell people how wonderful Jesus is!* And that is what I want to talk about. Every Christian has a story, a story of redemption and salvation and a story of a changed life. No one can become a Christian without his or her life being changed."

Warming up, he told the audience briefly about his early life and took them on his journey as a seaman and then told them about his life in New York City. They all listened respectfully. The crowd consisted mostly of Mennonites and also some Amish. When he first arrived, Ludlow had wondered where the "regular" Americans were, and then he was told that this was a huge Anabaptist community and that he would probably be speaking mostly to plain people.

Such a large group of Mennonites was new to him. He had visited Sunnyside Mennonite Church in Sarasota and shared his testimony there. In fact, he had decided to place his membership with the Sunnyside Church after he had moved to Florida.

Now he told the Ohio audience about his conversion experience. More than once people dabbed at their wet eyes as he told of his anguish of heart and then shared the joy of Jesus coming into his heart and giving him new life.

"Attending the Mennonite church in Hattieville gave me an understanding of what a blessing it is to belong to God's family. I learned so much from the brothers and sisters there. Remember how I told you about being told by God to call Miss Nancy? It was the joy she radiated earlier that made me think of her right then."

It was warm in the tent, but Ludlow did not mind. He was used to tropical weather, and his bandanna was readily available. Taking a sip of water from the glass on the podium, he continued, "I was baptized by Lester Gingerich in Belize. I wanted to express my love to God, and I wanted to have a public testimony of being a changed man through Jesus Christ."

Before starting the next part of his story, Ludlow paused for a moment. Gripping the edges of the podium with both hands, he said, "One of the biggest regrets of my life is that I lost my family. When my wife and children left me in Belize, it should have been a wake-up call for me. Instead, I simply threw myself into making money more than ever. When I decided to tear down Mopan, I wanted to get rid of anything that would hinder me from being restored to my wife and children. So I tore down the motel and decided to sell all my land. I had tried to sell Mopan, but there were no buyers. When I tried to sell the lots I still had, again there were no buyers. Finally I sold everything at bargain prices. What was worth thousands, I sold for hundreds until I had liquidated all my assets."

Outside the white tent darkness fell over the flat landscape. But Ludlow continued, "I had asked counsel from my Christian brothers and they understood what I was doing. Eventually I had only a travel trailer left, and I moved that onto Gilbert Steven's land and stayed there. But I had a plan. I wanted to be restored to my family. That was why I was willing to sell everything in Belize and come up here to be closer to my wife and children.

"You see, God has been working in Millicent's life too. After Dawn came back to the States, she willingly went to church with her mother. I see my family drawing closer to the Lord." Bowing his head slightly, Ludlow said, "Please pray for us. I am asking God to restore our marriage, and I believe He will." Unable to speak any further, he sat down.

As the meeting concluded, Ludlow sat with bowed head. Afterward people came up to him and sympathetically told him they would be praying for the restoration of his marriage and family. Ludlow thanked them all and was once again overwhelmed by the many brothers and sisters who said with tears, "Do not despair, brother. Keep on believing."

The motel was clean and comfortable, but it was not a home. Ludlow sat on the wooden chair and stared at the brown bedspread. "Oh, Lord, how long?" his anguished cry was wrenched from the depths of his heart. "How long must I wait?"

At first when he had moved into the Miami area to be close to Millicent and the children, hope and faith had surged high. He daily prayed for the restoration of his marriage, but he was busy traveling. From Pennsylvania, Indiana, Iowa, and Virginia, churches invited him to come and share his testimony. Ludlow traveled miles and miles, sometimes speaking in several churches on the same day.

Sometimes people asked probing questions. "Why did you not wait to sell your motel until a buyer came along? Was that good stewardship to let your assets dwindle away? Think of the money you could have had to help the poor."

To those occasional questions Ludlow would say, "When God asked me to get rid of the motel, all I wanted to do was to obey His voice. The earthly things were not important to me."

At times his answer satisfied the questioners, but at other times it brought more questions. "How did God speak to you? How do you know it was God and not your own reasoning?"

Trying to get people to understand, Ludlow would answer, "If you hear God speaking to you, you know it's Him. When the Spirit prompts you or speaks to your spirit, there is a connection. I firmly believe that God wanted me to tear down Mopan, not sell it."

He did meet people who understood. With beaming eyes and radiant smiles, they gave affirmation to what he was saying: "Yes, God speaks to us if we want to hear His voice."

The love offerings often overwhelmed him. Traveling was expensive and since he did not have a job, Ludlow depended on God for his finances. The motel was costly and yet he felt sure that God wanted him to live close to Millicent.

Now, in his motel room, only one thought stared him in the face: the restoration of his family. "Lord, I am happy to share my testimony with other people. Thank you for letting me glorify your name. But I am lonely. I know my former sins are forgiven, but they haunt me. I miss Millicent and my children. Oh, Lord, restore my family. Why must I continue to suffer?"

In the quietness that followed, Ludlow wept brokenly. From the beginning, right after his conversion, he had started sending money to Millicent to help her with the children. He knew she worked hard and long to provide for herself and the children.

She had told him how much she appreciated it. The first several meetings in Florida had been awkward, but they were seeing each other several times a week now. "Let me think about it," she would say whenever Ludlow would ask if she would consider living with him again.

Not wanting to be annoying, Ludlow had waited. He had seen the change in his wife's life and rejoiced. "I gave my life to the Lord Jesus too," she had told him. "Ludlow, both of the children and I have been baptized in our church."

Ludlow's heart had leaped with joy then, but now he kept pouring out his frustrations to God. "If we are both Christians, why are we still apart? I know it is not your will. You want our children to have both a father and a mother. Please, Lord, why are my prayers not answered?"

Barbara. Was it Millicent's mother who was keeping them apart? She had never really liked him, and after her daughter had left Ludlow, she had told Millicent she never wanted to see him again. Ludlow struggled with feelings against his mother-in-law. Why did she resist him so much? Both of her own marriages had failed. She now lived with Millicent, and Ludlow felt sure that daily she was trying to keep them apart.

Picking up his Bible, Ludlow tried to read. "Why could not we cast him out . . . this kind goeth not out but by prayer and fasting" (Matthew 17:19-21). The words seemed to leap from the page. Ludlow read them again. The disciples had not been able to cast the demon out of a young boy, and Jesus told them the reason for their failure.

"Lord, is that it?" Ludlow asked humbly. "Have I not had my prayers answered because I have not taken it seriously enough?"

Yes, I need to fast for our restoration. The thought hit him with startling clarity. Immediately, Ludlow felt humbled. God was speaking to him. He had been so busy traveling and sharing his testimony that even though he had kept on praying for his family, they had taken second place in his priorities. God was reminding him of that.

Weeping into his hands, Ludlow surrendered to the overwhelming love of Jesus for him. "You love me, Jesus. You want me to keep my focus on you and not on my traveling. I will fast for the restoration of my marriage. Lord, keep this need constantly in my mind."

CHAPTER 19

CUPS RUNNING OVER

Ludlow stood beside the motel window and stared blankly out into the hot Florida day that was ending with a final blast of heat. Even though his room was air-conditioned, Ludlow was sweating. The beads of moisture on his face were not because of the heat, however, but from the agony he was feeling.

Fast. That was what God had asked him to do. Fast to remove anything in his heart that was keeping Millicent from returning to him. Fast to allow the Spirit to have free movement in Millicent's heart and remove any hindrances that Satan was using to keep them from reuniting.

For five days Ludlow had fasted, spending time reading the Bible, praying for hours on his knees, and pacing back and forth in the motel room. At times the presence of God was very real and comforting. But at other times he had felt the enemy trying to bring all kinds of doubts and fears to his mind. Each day the battle seemed a little less severe, and Ludlow was finding the wonderful presence of his Father bringing peace and rest to his seeking heart.

"Lord, it is all yours—my life, Millicent's life, my children's lives. I give everything to you. My heart is warmed by your love, and more than anything, I rest in that. I can cast everything else aside because you have assured me over and over again that you will never leave me nor forsake me." Sometimes Ludlow prayed out loud, and at other times he prayed silently with "groanings which cannot be uttered."

Dimly he became aware of someone outside the motel room in the hall. It was not uncommon for guests to come and go. At first when he heard a quiet knock, Ludlow paid no attention to it. He thought the sound had come from another room. After all, no one came to see him here at this cheap motel. His meetings with Millicent always happened at her house.

But there it was again, a loud, firm knock. Puzzled, Ludlow went to the door. Could it be someone from housekeeping? Usually they came to clean the rooms in the morning when he was out.

"Who's there?" he asked cautiously.

A woman's voice answered, "Ludlow? It's Millicent."

Ludlow was utterly incapable of saying a word in reply. His usually deft fingers fumbled frantically with the lock. When he finally got the door open, the sight of Millicent looking up at him with her dark, luminous eyes nearly caused his knees to buckle. "May I come in?" she asked with a smile.

"Oh, yes, Millicent. Please come in." Ludlow stood to one side and Millicent walked in. Dazed, Ludlow closed the door behind her.

"Here, take this chair." Ludlow pushed forward the only chair in the room and seated Millicent beside the window. He stood in front of her, trembling. "Is everything all right?" he inquired anxiously. "The children?"

Millicent waved toward the bed, saying, "Sit down, Ludlow. Everything is all right. The children are fine. No, I actually came to tell you that if you still want to, I'm ready to take you back again."

Ludlow did not need an invitation to sit down. His knees buckled and he collapsed onto the edge of the bed. A chuckle escaped from somewhere deep inside him. "Millicent! How wonderful!" Wild emotions swirled in his chest, and he looked in disbelief at the beautiful woman he loved sitting so calmly on the chair. Just like that, she had walked in and told him she would take him back! It almost took his breath away.

"Praise God!" The words leaped from Ludlow's mouth. He reached out and took Millicent's hands in his own. "Oh, Millicent, how absolutely wonderful." He laughed out loud for sheer joy and Millicent joined him.

Ludlow was trying to wrap his mind around this wonderful news. How often before he had asked her to consider taking him back, but her answer had always been, "I'm not ready yet." Now she came to him and told him she was ready. How awesome!

"Your mother? Does she know? What will she say?" In spite of his joy, Ludlow felt a twinge of apprehension grip his heart.

Millicent looked down at her hands engulfed in Ludlow's strong hands. "I told her that if she didn't like it, she would have to find another place to live. I didn't tell her I was going to take you back until just before I came over here this evening, and I didn't even wait to see what she would say. I just told her and came right over here."

Once again, Ludlow laughed with joy. "What about the children? Do they know?"

"I haven't told them in so many words, but you know Dawn. I am sure she realizes what is happening, and Junior will be glad to have our family together again. Mother just has to make up her mind to accept it."

Ludlow knew that Millicent was completely convinced by now that he had made a radical change. She was willing to choose him even if it meant denying her mother's wishes. Oh, how that thought thrilled him. "How soon?" he asked eagerly.

Millicent smiled up at him. "Just as soon as we can arrange it," she whispered. "I want Pastor Jim to marry us, Ludlow, if that is all right. He is the one who baptized Dawn and Junior and me. I don't want anyone except just our family and Jim and Angela. After all, this is not the first wedding."

Ludlow nodded enthusiastically. "Oh, yes, Millicent. To renew our vows will be a sacred and holy time. Yet, I agree, it needs to be only the family and Jim and Angela. Speak to them as soon as you can."

In spite of his immense joy, Ludlow felt constrained to say soberly, "Millicent, I am deeply honored to have you accept me into your life and heart again, and yet I feel God wants me to ask your mother's approval for our wedding. Even though I am so happy that you first came to me with your answer, I want to respect your mother and ask for your hand once more."

"And if she refuses?" Millicent asked.

"Then we will have to ask God once again for direction. I don't know how, but I do believe He can remove even that obstacle."

They made some more plans and prayed together before Millicent left to go back to the children. Ludlow could hardly contain his joy and spent wonderful hours with Jesus, weeping with joy and lifting his heart in adoration to the Lord for His wonderful workings.

"Barbara, I have something to ask of you," Ludlow said respectfully. The children had gone outside after their dinner together. All evening he had been trying to read Barbara's mind. Was she slightly friendlier toward him than before? Did she seem to be reconciled to her daughter's decision?

"Yes, Ludlow?" Her question was expressionless, void of emotion.

"Yes, ma'am," he continued, "I want to ask your permission and blessing for Millicent and me to get married again." Wisely, Ludlow made no elaborate promises or even claims of being a changed person. He simply asked for her permission with respect and dignity, and he knew that God could do more to move her heart than any persuasive eloquence on his part.

"Once more you ask for my daughter's hand. Well, Ludlow, you have not always been welcome in my life, but I can see that you have changed. I have no objections," Barbara said with a shrug of her shoulders.

Ludlow felt humbled as a wave of gratitude swept over him. How good God was! He had imagined all kinds of accusations and reluctance from Barbara as he had imagined this moment again and again. Now she had not only dropped her objections, but she actually seemed glad to have their family reunited.

Looking from Barbara to Millicent with his broadest smile, Ludlow reached out and shook his mother-in-law's hand gratefully. "Thank you," he said from the depth of his heart.

Rising from her seat, Barbara said, "I will leave you two alone, for I know you have plans to complete." Without further words she went into her bedroom.

Ludlow drew Millicent up from her chair and into his arms. It took all his effort to keep his feet from dancing. "Millicent, how good God is! How marvelously He has worked out everything. We can move ahead with the plans to renew our vows!"

October in Homestead, Florida, is often warm and humid, but inside Jim and Angela Smith's house, the air conditioner kept everything cool and pleasant. There was something more than air conditioning, though, that made this day pleasant. October 9, 1982, would always stand out in Ludlow's mind as one of the greatest days of his life—the day his family was reunited. It was the day he had longed and prayed for ever since his conversion.

"Ludlow and Millicent, do you pledge yourselves to follow God for the rest of your lives, obey His commandments, and live together in marriage for as long as you both shall live?"

Ludlow and Millicent were standing in the living room at the home of Millicent's pastor. Dawn and Ludlow Junior, dressed in their best clothes, stood beside their parents. Angela stood beside her husband, beaming with happiness. From the beginning Jim and Angela had longed to see this family reunited, and now they were rejoicing with their friends as Ludlow and Millicent renewed their vows.

"Ludlow, do you take Millicent, this woman by your side, as your lawfully wedded wife for as long as you both shall live?"

"I do," Ludlow said firmly, gazing into Millicent's eyes.

"Millicent, do you take Ludlow Walker, this man by your side, as your lawfully wedded husband for as long as you both shall live?"

"I do," Millicent echoed, smiling at her husband.

"May the Lord Jesus Christ, who has blessed this union with two beautiful children, restore this marriage," Pastor Smith prayed as they joined hands. "May the name of Jesus be glorified for the redemptive work He has done. May people everywhere give glory and praise to the One who has done such marvelous works in this family. God, I pray that they would work together and that many, many hearts would come to know you because of their walk and their testimony."

After the ceremony Angela ushered them into the dining room. There she had prepared a feast and the happy family sat down with their hosts.

"Ludlow, would you ask the blessing?" Pastor Smith asked.

Ludlow's heart was so full that for a long time he could say nothing. Finally he prayed, and his words reflected deep thankfulness to God, first of all for their salvation in Jesus, and then for His goodness in reuniting them.

"Bless all our dear friends who have never stopped praying for us, Lord. Bless them for their faithfulness and for their caring hearts. Amen."

Ludlow and Millicent both knew that in the days ahead there would be adjustments for both of them as well as for their children. Millicent had been the head of the family for four years, and it would not be easy for the children to get used to having Ludlow take his role as a leader once again. They were honest enough to acknowledge that the damage done by their broken marriage would not be healed without some growing pains. Yet, the same God who had brought them back together again would surely also give them the grace to meet each challenge and obstacle with humility and mutual respect. Both Ludlow and Millicent were confident that God's Spirit would guide them into a new life of selfless love.

And so they ate together. They visited and laughed. They were a family, reunited by their Lord and deeply grateful to Him.

AGAPE AUTO
WASH AND WAX

The traffic whizzed past the gas station located on Highway 1 south of Miami. This had long been largely undeveloped land except for the strip along the highway that led to the Florida Keys. Now, in the late 1980s, developers were buying up land, and speculators came by the droves to build homes for people wanting to enjoy the tropical climate.

"This is where I will be detailing the cars," Ludlow told the county permit officer.

The inspector said very little as he walked around the space indicated and made notes on his clipboard. Ludlow waited. "Lord, please move in his heart to grant me the permit. I want this business to be a door into the community for your glory."

Always the entrepreneur, Ludlow had taken the challenge of selling ads for a Christian radio station. At first it had been difficult to sell advertising, but even after the business owners began placing ads, Ludlow felt God wanted him to do something else.

That was when the vision to do auto detailing had been birthed. He felt it was a sign from God that the first gas station owner he had approached was willing to lease a space at the side of the lot for the auto detailing business he wanted to open.

"When did you erect the tent?" Ludlow's thoughts returned to the present as he heard the inspector's voice.

"On Tuesday, two days ago," he replied. Once more the inspector made a careful inspection of the canopy-like structure. He pushed against one of the metal posts holding up the canvas. Then he walked over to the storm drain and measured it, recording the dimensions.

Rising to his feet, the inspector signed the sheet, tore it off, and handed it to Ludlow, saying crisply, "I cannot approve your application."

Ludlow looked at the page. Arthur Smanski, Inspector. Both signed and printed.

"Mr. Smanski, I put a lot of thought and study into this venture," Ludlow spoke respectfully. "I interviewed several other auto detailers in South Florida, and my situation here is almost identical to at least two others."

Mr. Smanski held up one hand, palm facing Ludlow. "I am sorry, but the drainage system here is not designed to handle the large quantities of water released by a car wash. Your application is rejected."

Ludlow tried once more. "I don't understand. Auto detailing is different from a car wash. There is not a large amount of water used for each car."

"How many gallons?"

Ludlow shook his head. "I don't know exactly," he admitted. "I forgot to ask any of the other detail shop owners. But I can find out."

The inspector shrugged and turned to walk to his truck.

"Sir, can you give me a reason why my application is denied while others have permits to operate a detail shop in situations almost identical to mine? It doesn't make sense." Ludlow tried to keep the frustration out of his voice.

The inspector said nothing and climbed into his cab.

"Mr. Smanski, where is your office located, please? I want to appeal this decision."

"The address is on the inspection report," Mr. Smanski replied, nodding toward the paper in Ludlow's hand. He slammed the door of his truck, started the engine, merged into the flow of traffic, and disappeared.

Ludlow noted the address on the report: 2314 South Main Street. Turning, he surveyed his proposed business site once again. It had seemed so ideal. Right along the highway, with wonderful visibility to southbound traffic, alongside the gas station, which would give him a lot of exposure to local customers . . . it had all seemed so right when he had prayed about it.

"Why would I get a green light from the Lord if now the door is closed?" Ludlow wondered out loud. Bowing his head, he began to pray.

Clutching his carefully drawn proposal for Agape Auto Wash and Wax, Ludlow parked his car in the downtown Miami parking garage. Checking the address once more, he crossed on a pedestrian walkway and reached the sidewalk crowded with people. Rolling black clouds darkened the sky above him, and the winds sent people scurrying along. A thunderstorm was about to explode on them. Perhaps it would bring the temperatures down out of the nineties and bring a much needed reprieve from the Florida heat. Ludlow mopped his forehead repeatedly. He checked his watch. Good. Thirty minutes early.

The receptionist on the telephone had finally scheduled an appointment for him to meet with the correct department. "Make sure you are on time," she had told him with a tone that clearly implied that she was granting him a favor. "Mr. Blalock is a very busy man."

Two o'clock in the afternoon had been fine with Ludlow. If his appointment wouldn't take too long, he knew he should be out of the city before the evening rush of traffic clogged the highway south into Homestead. But before he reached the twelve-story building where the office was located, the thunderstorm broke loose. Lightning and thunder simultaneously shot and rolled out of the skies and the winds whipped around the corners. Rain began to fall in sheets and Ludlow ran the last hundred yards to the shelter of the overhang in front of the building.

As lightning crackled in the air and thunder shook the ground, the pedestrians all hurried inside any available shelter. Another barrage of lightning and thunder flashed onto the city, and the brightly lit buildings were plunged into darkness as the electricity went off.

Ludlow had just entered the lobby when that building was plunged into darkness and he heard a woman squealing in fright. The elevator lights blinked and emergency lighting came on, creating an eerie glow in the interior.

"Don't use the elevators!" someone yelled.

Ludlow was trying to get his bearing in the melee. He checked his paper. Fifth floor. He looked for the staircase and headed in that direction. As he ascended the stairs, he met dozens of office workers scurrying down the steps, all chattering nervously.

"First of all they run inside when the storm breaks, and now they all run outside when the power goes off," a level-headed gentlemen remarked, ascending the steps with Ludlow.

Ludlow chuckled. "It's not as if these storms don't hit us every summer. I would think people would eventually get used to them."

The corridor outside the Planning and Zoning Division was largely deserted. Windows at each end of the hall let in some light and emergency exit lights shone above the staircase doors at each end.

Suite 112, the paper said. Ludlow tried the door and it opened. The office was deserted.

"Hello!" Ludlow called loudly.

From an inner office a man appeared, holding a sheet of paper. Outside, the storm still raged. "I have an appointment at two o'clock to appeal a decision made by Inspector Smanski," Ludlow spoke slowly, letting his words sink in.

The man looked vacantly at Ludlow for a minute as though trying to understand how this involved him. He looked at the vacant desks in the reception room. "Where is Sally?" he asked in a bewildered voice.

"Probably in the main lobby on the first floor," Ludlow said with a grin. "I saw an awful lot of people hurrying down the stairs to escape the storm."

For a brief moment Ludlow's humor registered with the man and a half-smile flitted across his tired features. Then briskly taking control again, he ordered, "Wait here for a moment. There has been an emergency and we are waiting for the backup generator to provide full power."

Ludlow nodded and found a seat. The man disappeared into his office again. As the floor beneath him trembled from another mighty roll of thunder, Ludlow recalled the thunderstorm in Belize that had frightened him and sent him running down the road. "I guess I am not that different from many others, Lord," he said under his breath. "Except now you have removed my fear and assured me that I never need to be alone or afraid."

Suddenly the lights flickered and the power was restored. "Right this way, Mr. Walker." The man had reappeared and Ludlow followed him into a large room.

"Yes?" The man at the desk looked up wearily as Ludlow approached him.

"I am Ludlow Walker and I have an appointment at two o'clock to appeal a rejection for a permit to operate Agape Auto Wash and Wax."

"I'm Stephen Blalock. Take a seat." The man nodded at Ludlow and then glanced out the window as the rain lashed against the glass. "Whew, that's some storm." Returning his attention to the matter at hand, he murmured, "Agape Auto Wash and Wax. That's an unusual name." He looked with interest at the tall Jamaican.

Ludlow sat down and handed his papers across the desk to Mr. Blalock. Another furious assault of lightning and thunder shook the building. The lights blinked but stayed on.

"I was denied a permit because the inspector who surveyed the site told me the storm sewers weren't adequate for a car wash. I told him we would only be washing cars by hand and that the runoff water would be minimal."

"About how many cars will you be able to do a day, Mr. Walker?"

"The most would be twelve a day. It takes almost an hour to properly wash, wax, and detail each vehicle. The total amount of water used for each vehicle will be under twenty gallons," Ludlow said. He waited while the chief inspector studied his proposal.

"That will be a very small daily amount even if there are twelve cars," Mr. Blalock mused aloud. Looking over the rejection sheet he asked, "Who refused your application?"

"Mr. Arthur Smanski."

Turning in his chair, Mr. Blalock called, "Arthur, are you in there?"

Mr. Smanski appeared. "Yes, sir?" He looked at Ludlow, then at his superior.

"On what grounds did you deny Mr. Walker's request for a permit to operate his auto wash and wax?"

"Storm drains are not able to handle a large capacity of water according to Volume 5, Section 6 of the county codes."

"Where is the application? Get it and bring it here. Arthur, this man is applying for an auto detailing station, not a car wash with huge amounts of water flushing into the drains. There is a big difference." With a flourish Mr. Blalock signed Ludlow's application and stamped the approval onto the document.

"Where is Sally? I have pressed her bell over and over and no one answers." Mr. Blalock frowned at his pile of papers.

"The storm has sent most of the people scurrying," Ludlow said as he stood up. "Before I leave, I need to tell you about something that happened to me once during a storm."

Briefly he recounted the happening in Belize. "I learned a valuable lesson that day, Mr. Blalock. I do not need to fear the storm. It is a reminder to me that the One who created the storm is in perfect control, not only of the universe, but also of my life."

"You mean to tell me you are the one who caused this storm today?" Mr. Blalock asked with a twinkle in his eyes.

"No, sir," Ludlow chuckled, "but I do believe God sent this storm today to get Sally out of the office so you could hear my story directly."

As another flash of lightning lit the sky outside the window, Mr. Blalock chuckled. "Maybe you are right, because people usually have to wait several hours to get past Sally. She books people ahead of time because I have such a busy schedule."

Clutching his documents, Ludlow left with a light heart. "You did it again, Lord. Thank you for the thunderstorms!"

"Is it okay, young man, if I wait until you are done? You say it will take forty-five minutes?" The elderly lady clutched her purse to her blouse.

"Oh, yes, ma'am," Manuel said kindly. "Mr. Walker put those chairs there for just that purpose. May I get you a cup of coffee while you get settled?"

Samantha Weinbrunner smiled and said, "That would be wonderful. You are a polite young man."

Manuel flashed a sunny smile at his customer and filled a Styrofoam cup with the hot steaming liquid from the coffee maker. "Cream or sugar?" he inquired.

The powder blue Cadillac sat under the awning. Manuel started on the inside, carefully washing the dash, vacuuming the carpets, and paying attention to the smallest detail, all under the scrutiny of Mrs. Weinbrunner.

"Well, I guess it has a good name, detail shop," Mrs. Weinbrunner said as she picked up a magazine. "You sure are getting all the details."

Ludlow parked his truck and walked over to where Manuel was working. "Hey, Manuel, it looks like you have everything under control."

"Yes, sir," Manuel smiled at his boss. "This one and then two more this afternoon."

Ludlow nodded.

"How was your trip north?" Manuel asked, reaching for a clean cloth.

"It went well," Ludlow said. "I spoke at five churches and the people were very receptive. God blessed my journey."

"Are you the owner?" asked Mrs. Weinbrunner, who had been listening in on the conversation.

"Yes, ma'am. I'm Ludlow Walker." He shook the lady's hand.

"Well, I must say you run a fine little detailing shop here," Mrs. Weinbrunner said approvingly. "That young man is most polite and he is doing a good job too. I am watching."

Ludlow smiled. "Yes, Manuel has been with me for four years and he is a good worker."

"Why do you call it Agape? What does love have to do with cars?"

Ludlow sat down on a chair. "Love has something to do with everything, ma'am. Even car detailing."

"I guess it helps people trust you," was his customer's comment.

"I want all people to know of the love Jesus Christ has shown to me," Ludlow said pleasantly. "I chose to call it Agape to let people know that I am experiencing the love of Jesus and that I will extend the service a follower of His should give. Do you know His love, ma'am?"

"I am Jewish," Mrs. Weinbrunner said stiffly, as though that should end the conversation.

"You know, my grandfather was a Jew. That makes us some kind of kin, doesn't it?" Ludlow said with a smile.

"Your grandfather? But you are . . ."

"Black," Ludlow finished for her. "My grandmother was a Jamaican and so I have both Jewish and Jamaican heritage. But as proud as I am of my heritage, I still consider myself most blessed to be loved by Jesus and to have Him in my life. You know, ma'am, Jesus came to the world for all people, regardless of nationality, race, or class. He was a Jew Himself, you remember."

"This is a most unusual combination of faiths and cultures. How did you come to believe in this man you call Jesus?" Mrs. Weinbrunner asked with genuine interest.

As Ludlow shared his testimony and answered the woman's questions, Manuel efficiently washed, waxed, and polished the blue Cadillac. He nodded several times as he listened to Ludlow speak passionately about what had happened to him.

This was not the first time this had happened. Even though Manuel knew the story of how his boss had become a Christian, he was always blessed by the way Ludlow used every opportunity to talk to people about their need for Jesus. Numerous times Ludlow had connected with fellow believers too, and the little canopy had sheltered prayer meetings and testimonies of praise and worship.

Manuel had been pleased to find such a good job working for a Christian boss. It had helped him a lot in his own walk with the Lord.

He gave a final polish to the gleaming exterior and then approached Mrs. Weinbrunner. "All finished, ma'am," he said with a smile.

"What? Done already? I thought forty-five minutes would go slowly, but the time just flew." Turning to Ludlow, she said, "Your story is most interesting. I see it made a big impact on your life to have God speak to you."

"It was all through Jesus," Ludlow reminded her gently.

"Oh, yes." The woman stood up. "How much do I owe you?"

As the blue Cadillac drove off, Ludlow told Manuel, "I'll help you with the next car. You may take a break until the following customer shows up."

"Thank you, sir," Manuel said gratefully. "And it's good to have you back from your trip."

21

WIPED OUT

"I am hearing from the Lord that I am to close Agape." Ludlow's words hung in midair, suspended in the stunned silence that followed his words to Millicent. Even to Ludlow, it sounded ridiculous. The idea made no sense.

Millicent echoed his own doubts with an incredulous, "What has been added to your lemonade?" They both laughed at the comment, but then she sobered. "Why would God be asking you to shut down Agape? For the last six years it has been doing well, and you do realize that the business is making the house payments."

Ludlow nodded. He had no explanation.

Millicent waited. She had learned to not be hasty with her questions, but allow Ludlow to explain to her what he was sensing. How different this man was from the Ludlow she had first known. Back then, he had always seemed so sure of himself. He knew just where he wanted to go in the world and pursued business strategies regardless of how they affected anyone around him. Now he was softer, more in touch with how his choices would affect his relationship with his family and with God.

Shaking his head, Ludlow said slowly, "I feel so strongly about this. I am not sure if God is preparing me to have even more speaking engagements, to be gone more from home, or what. But I have this growing awareness that God is asking me to close down Agape. I want nothing but God's will in this, so I am praying for a sign from Him. Something that will give me a clear understanding of His will."

They both waited in the silence. The significance of the decision was not lost on them. Gone were the days when money had flowed painlessly from his bank account. Now they lived from month to month, making their payments, providing for their children's needs, and living frugally. Their house was mortgaged, their car was an older model, but even though they were not rich, they were comfortable. To quit a steady income could mean an abrupt change from what they were enjoying.

"I know if God is asking you to do this, it will be okay," Millicent said softly.

Ludlow looked at his wife and a slow smile spread across his face. "Thank you," he said sincerely, appreciating the treasure of his wife's support.

Much had happened in their years together after they had been reunited. Their love for God had grown, and as they had walked in the love of God, their marriage relationship had become better and better. True, they were still a work in progress, but they were growing.

"You won't worry?" Ludlow asked. "I know it is not easy to fully trust God to supply our needs, but right now, that is what I feel He wants us to do."

"I trust Him, but really, sometimes I don't trust myself," Millicent said. "My faith may be strong today, but what about tomorrow?"

Ludlow nodded sympathetically. "Me too," he acknowledged. "But as I continue to pray for a sign, I will also continue to trust."

"What all did they take?" Ludlow asked wearily.

Manuel lifted his shoulders and spread out his hands, saying, "Everything they could steal: the power washer, the vacuum cleaners, the buffers and polishers, the cleaners. They even took the air fresheners we usually hang on rearview mirrors. If it was not a part of the building, they took it."

Ludlow rubbed the top of his head thoughtfully. "How many appointments do we have today?"

Manuel checked the schedule. "Just one this afternoon," he said slowly.

"Just one?" Ludlow asked in dismay. "This doesn't look good."

"Boss, the business has continued to slack off," Manuel said as he kicked at the bottom of the trash can. "This is funny. Why didn't they take the trash can?" He laughed his usual sunny laugh, but sobered up immediately.

"Something is going on," Ludlow said slowly, looking once more at the stripped storage room. "Something strange is happening." After analyzing the situation, he finally decided, "I will bring some supplies from home and buy the rest. I'll be back after lunch. Perhaps a drive-in customer will come. Call me if you need me."

The short drive to his home gave Ludlow a chance to try to piece together what was happening. Just the week before last he had found himself at the bank, withdrawing from his savings to pay Manuel and the other part-time helper. His customer base seemed to be drying up. This had concerned him as he had left for a trip north and spent days traveling and speaking at churches, sharing his testimony and preaching to receptive audiences. Now he had come home to this.

Merging into the southbound traffic, Ludlow felt there was something trying to get through to him. "Lord, what is it?" he asked sincerely.

"I am speaking to you," the voice of God responded in his heart.

Ludlow passed a slow-moving dump truck loaded with gravel. He swung back into the right lane. Was God actually speaking to him through the thieves? Through the loss of customers? What was He trying to tell him?

"It's your business. It's time to shut down Agape."

That message again? He was to get rid of a business that was making his house payments? How was he to make a living? True, the love offerings from the churches sometimes did amount to quite a bit more than his travel expenses, but not always. He couldn't depend on those alone, could he?

"Trust me."

Trust. How often Ludlow had asked God for a greater measure of faith and trust to be able to totally depend on the Lord for all his needs. Yes, that was what he had often prayed. At times he thought about how he had liquidated his assets in Belize. If he had only held out, would God have sent a buyer for Mopan? Or maybe he could have sold those lots for several thousand dollars instead of only for hundreds. Perhaps he would have had enough to buy a house outright, leaving him more freedom to be involved in kingdom work.

As he neared home, the battle still raged in his mind. Pulling into his drive, Ludlow stopped the engine. "Lord, just give me the faith I need," he implored. "Give me the sign from you." A sign. He remembered suddenly that he had asked God for a sign about six months ago.

Now as he reflected on his business, Ludlow realized it was about six months ago that he had begun to notice his business slacking off. Very slowly at first, and then more often than not, there was no profit at the end of the week. For a few weeks, a slight gain would reassure him, but yes, the decline was getting more and more pronounced.

"You wanted a sign. Well, your equipment is gone."

Ludlow stared straight ahead and yet saw nothing. His mind was racing. *That downward slump in business. The sudden increase in speaking engagements. The multiple opportunities to minister through the local Southmost Mennonite Church where they attended. And finally, the robbery.*

"I get the message, Lord," Ludlow said. "Forgive my unbelief. I will close down the business. I will trust in you, Lord."

A load seemed to lift off Ludlow as he opened the car door and went to tell Millicent.

———————————————

"Push it up a little higher," Ludlow called out to his son from his perch on the stepladder. The evening air on that hot, humid summer evening of late August 1992 was silent except for the sound of hammers banging away throughout their neighborhood.

"Two more to go," Ludlow Junior said, brushing his hands together. "There sure doesn't seem to be anything in the weather to justify the dire forecasts."

Ludlow climbed down from the stepladder and looked toward the south. In the waning light, he could see nothing out of the ordinary.

"Let's get those other two windows boarded up in case the storm does hit," he said. The two completed the job and then went inside where the cheery lights shone from the lamps in the living room.

"Do you have your jugs filled with drinking water?" Barbara Dennings asked, rubbing her hands over the armchair where she was sitting. "I just don't know what to expect."

"They say Andrew could be a category six hurricane," Ludlow Junior commented, sprawling his eighteen-year-old body on the sofa. "That would be one serious storm."

"Well, we don't know yet how severe the storm will be," Millicent said, handing her mother a glass of iced tea. "Maybe it will blow around us."

"We pray that the storm will stay in the ocean, but all indications are that it will hit somewhere in South Florida," Ludlow said. "We must get ready for whatever the Lord sends."

"Well, we have enough bread and milk to last for several days," Millicent said. "The lines of people at the grocery store were long and almost everyone had the same items in their carts. Milk and bread were the top sellers."

"Do the stores have a surplus of milk and bread after the storms pass?" Ludlow Junior asked with a chuckle. "If everyone buys up bread and milk before the storm, there must be a period of time afterwards when those items aren't needed."

They all laughed. Ludlow Junior could be counted on to bring humor into a tense situation. "Probably there will be lots of plywood for sale afterward too," he continued, "unless people hang on to it for the next storm."

"The wind is rising," Ludlow commented, going to the front door and looking out through the glass. The palm tree across the street was beginning to bend and sway.

"Flashlights are on the hall table," Millicent told them on her way into the kitchen. She could see lights in the neighbor's living room. Their house faced east, the direction the storm was coming from.

"There goes a limb," Ludlow said from his post by the front door.

Ludlow Junior came to stand beside his father. "The awning on the Johnsons' house is taking a beating," he observed.

At first there was no rain, only wind, but then in the glow from the street lights, the watchers could see rain being driven horizontally and hitting the side of the house under the front porch.

The first twenty minutes of storm were no worse than other hurricanes the Walkers had experienced in their ten years together in Florida. More than once they had waited out the hours of wind and later repaired the minor damages inflicted by the storms. Perhaps this one would blow itself out in several hours as well.

But the intensity of the wind grew. Above the loud roar of the wind, Ludlow could hear large objects being hurled against the house and onto the roof. Suddenly the lights blinked and they were plunged into darkness.

Barbara cried out in alarm and Millicent switched on a flashlight. The dim circle made a curious spot of light. "Here, Mother, you keep a hold on this light," Millicent said reassuringly. "I'll get the other one."

"It does sound like a freight train right outside the door," Ludlow Junior yelled above the noise.

Once more Ludlow tried to look out the front door, but just as he reached it, the tremendous crash of an object slamming against the door made him change his mind. "Time to get together in the bathroom," he yelled, taking Millicent by the hand. Located in the middle of the house, the bathroom had earlier been chosen as the safest place to ride out the storm. All the bulletins put out by the Safety Advisory Board recommended taking refuge in a small inner room. The risk of having the ceiling collapse in a small bathroom was far less than in a larger area such as the living room.

Millicent had placed the couch cushions outside in the hall, and they now carried those into the bathroom. Ludlow closed the door and the noise of the storm grew muffled.

"I hope Dawn doesn't worry about us," Millicent said, her thoughts drawn to her daughter studying in New York.

"I hope she is praying for us," Barbara said, sitting uneasily on the edge of the tub.

"Here, Mother, sit on this stack of cushions." Millicent shone her flashlight into the corner. "You can rest against the vanity if the drawer handles don't poke into your back."

A wrenching sound above them shocked them into silence. No one spoke as the sound of the thumps and blows on the roof came right through the ceiling to their terrified ears.

"Is the roof coming off?" Barbara shouted. Millicent wrapped a blanket around her mother's shaking shoulders.

"Oh, Lord, save our house. Have mercy on us and on our city." Ludlow was praying out loud, his words barely audible above the storm.

His thoughts went to the rest of the people from their church. Was everyone safe? Probably some had gone to seek safety in a storm shelter. The city officials had recommended everyone to evacuate and seek shelter in approved places, but Ludlow had not wanted to leave his home. Too often thieves took the opportunity to loot and pillage homes when they knew the inhabitants had sought shelter elsewhere.

As the storm continued to pound their house, Ludlow's thoughts went back to the two years since he had closed down Agape Auto Wash and Wax. God had provided for all their needs. The mortgage payments on the house had been paid, their daily living needs were met, and even though Ludlow continued to travel and speak at crusades and meetings, they had not suffered.

"Lord, you did it all," Ludlow prayed gratefully, fighting off the fear that wanted to grip him as he thought of the devastation this storm was causing. He knew very well that not only was his house being bombarded, but also all the houses in Homestead. He had no idea how far north toward Miami the storm was raging.

The gale continued to roar unabated. Ludlow was sure at least part of the roof was torn off. He hoped it was just the shingles.

All at once the noise died down and an eerie silence fell.

"Eye of the hurricane," Ludlow Junior remarked briefly from his place in the bathtub. "More will follow."

Ludlow opened the door and flashed the light into the hall. He checked his watch. Midnight. That meant they had endured three hours of gales during the first half of the massive storm. Could their house possibly withstand three more hours of that wind? Ludlow shook his head doubtfully as he went out the back door, followed by his son.

Going around the side of the house, they stepped over scattered branches and debris submerged in puddles. Rain still fell from the darkness overhead. Other pools of light flashed around the neighbors' yards as people emerged to assess the damage.

Voices called out in the darkness, and it was reassuring to hear people speaking. The absence of the roaring wind was an enormous relief to those who had chosen to ride out the storm in their homes.

"I hear it coming again," Ludlow yelled as the menacing roar came sweeping toward them once more. They dashed inside and huddled in the bathroom for the second time.

"How was it?" Millicent yelled.

"Couldn't see very much—too dark," bellowed Ludlow.

When the house shook once more under the onslaught of the hurricane, Ludlow began singing.

> Hold me fast, let me stand
> In the hollow of your hand.
> Keep me safe, till the storm passes by.

The others joined in, but it was hard to sing above the noise. Once more Ludlow began to pray and he could hear the voices of the others as they joined in calling on God for protection.

There were tremendous thumps outside and the agonizing sound of boards being wrenched away from the house. After one incredible gust of wind (later estimated to be over 120 miles an hour) there was the sound of splintering glass. The door of the bathroom shook and air swept in under the door.

"Oh, Lord, have mercy," Ludlow prayed, fearing for their safety. No longer was his concern for the house to remain undamaged—he was praying for their lives! He should at least have taken his wife and mother-in-law to the storm shelter!

"Water is coming from the ceiling!" Ludlow Junior shouted. "The roof must be gone!"

"Get out of the tub!" Ludlow shouted, shining a beam of light upward.

"Make sure the drain is open!" With creaks and groans, the walls heaved in the wind and tremors shook the floor under their feet.

Millicent huddled beside her mother, covering their heads with the blanket, and Ludlow stood with his arm across his son's shoulders. For the next two hours, they prayed urgently for their own safety and for the safety of the people in the path of the devastating storm.

CHAPTER 22

OUT OF THE WRECKAGE

The residents of South Florida emerged after Hurricane Andrew, devastated and bewildered by scenes of destruction on a scale they had never imagined. In Dade County alone, 90 percent of the homes sustained anything from serious roof damage to complete destruction. Overall, more than 110,000 homes were completely destroyed or suffered major damage from Andrew. Amazingly, the death toll was quite low, considering the 300,000 people who were left homeless and had to move into temporary quarters provided by the government or by caring friends and family members.

Ludlow helped his family out of the battered remains of their house. As they surveyed all the damaged homes up and down their street, they were speechless. It felt like they were standing in a gigantic landfill where trash and debris of every description was scattered all around them. Toppled trees now lay strewn where graceful palm trees and landscaped lawns had once adorned the homes. The few trees that survived the storm were stripped clear of their branches. Cars that had been parked on the streets were either turned on their sides or sat askew where the violent winds had pushed them. There was no pattern to which way the roofs had crashed or how the trees had toppled. Random scenes of destruction and chaos were everywhere.

Millicent covered her mouth and moaned at the sight. "Where are all the people?" she managed to whisper at last. Here and there a few figures could be seen moving around the scene of devastation, but not many.

"I guess many were wiser than we were and evacuated to storm shelters," Ludlow said. "Oh, Lord, have mercy on us!"

Later when they found out that Hurricane Andrew's winds had reached speeds of 175 miles an hour, they marveled that anything at all was left standing. But in the aftermath of the storm, statistics meant little to them. Their immediate concern was for the safety of their neighbors. How many people had actually perished in the storm? What was the next step for them? How could their lives continue amid all this wreckage? How could they ever rebuild? Should they even try to rebuild? What if they rebuilt, only to have another hurricane devastate them again?

Ludlow felt bewildered. There were too many questions, too many unknowns. "Oh, God, we need your help!" he prayed desperately as he surveyed the desolation around him. "Please, God, you have spared our lives and for that we are truly grateful. Now we look to you for the next step. Please give us your guidance and direction."

"Leroy! Over here!" Ludlow heard the shout from one of the construction workers. Rising hastily from his seat in the little travel trailer, he kicked the small table beside him.

"Sorry," he apologized to Millicent, bending down to repair the damage. "I keep forgetting it is there."

"It's the only place I can think of to keep the books," Millicent said from the other side of the tiny table, folded down from the wall to accommodate their breakfast.

"It's better than most people have," Ludlow replied gratefully, as he went to the small door and opened it. He stooped to exit the travel trailer and waved at the workers who were already donning their tool pouches.

"Good morning! May the Lord bless you," he called to the volunteers. A cheerful chorus of greetings came back from the workers. Mahlon Diller, the coordinator, approached Ludlow.

"Your workers did a great job yesterday," Ludlow greeted the middle-aged man. "I figured it would take at least a week before the roof would be on, much less all the shingles put down."

"Yes, praise God, we have very willing and ready workers," Mahlon laughed. "They like to work fast, and when you get workers from different carpenter crews together, it quickly becomes a contest to see who can be the most efficient." Seven men and teen-aged boys were already swarming about, busy putting the sheathing around the reconstructed house.

"Your house was easier to do than some," Mahlon remarked as they stood side by side and watched the group at work. "We were pleased to find most of the walls still standing and we could build from there."

"I don't know what the insurance company will do," Ludlow told his new friend, furrowing his brow. "I, along with thousands of others, have sent in my claim. Who knows when, or if, they will ever get around to really helping us."

Mahlon nodded. "Hurricane Andrew will go down in history as a particularly destructive storm," he said. "I hear story after story of its devastation, and just driving through this area makes me realize what a path of destruction this storm has cut across Dade County."

"Those of us who merely lost our homes are the more fortunate," Ludlow said thoughtfully. "Those who lost family members are the ones who are suffering the most." Both men fell silent as they thought of the lives Hurricane Andrew had claimed. Finally Ludlow began to pray. "Lord, bless the sorrowing families with your peace." Mahlon bowed his head in heartfelt agreement.

As is always the case after a massive storm, the infrastructure of a community is under massive stress. Much time is needed for the people to clean up and decide how to move on. Indeed, in this case, the landscape around them was so severely altered that many people found it difficult to find their way home after the storm. Landmarks were destroyed, homes were gone, and piles of rubbish and debris lined the streets, waiting to be hauled away by the city government.

"When we came out of our house the day after the hurricane, it was as though time had stopped," Ludlow told Mahlon. "Trash and debris were everywhere and the trees that were still standing looked as though a giant egg beater had whipped them unmercifully. Our first concern was naturally for the safety of our neighbors. We met a few of them in the streets, and although there were several scratches and cuts, no one here was killed or even seriously injured." The emotions of the memories choked Ludlow and for a moment he could not speak.

Mahlon reached out and laid a sympathetic hand on Ludlow's shoulder.

"When our Mennonite brothers from Sarasota heard of our situation," Ludlow continued, "they immediately brought this travel trailer down and we were able to move into it. Small as it is, it is better than staying in a crowded motel. Then those brothers offered to come and help us rebuild. Right after that you came from Christian Aid Ministries in Ohio and brought volunteers. God is really using you folks to be a witness and testimony in this area."

"We were really touched by the hardships that all of you here in South Florida suffered," Mahlon replied. "It is a privilege to be able to help."

A volley of laughter rose from the back of the house. A moment later, a young man came dashing around the side of the house, followed by a friend in good-natured pursuit.

"Not only do you folks bring help, you bring a sense of joy and happiness back into our lives," chuckled Ludlow. "It means so much just to hear laughter again."

Mahlon smiled indulgently at the young pranksters. "Yes, they certainly do know how to enjoy themselves," he agreed.

"Last Sunday evening was really special," Ludlow continued, turning to Mahlon again. "You don't know how much we appreciated the songs and prayers from your group. Our congregation was deeply moved by the sight of your group singing and encouraging our people."

"We have come in the name of Jesus," Mahlon said simply as he turned to walk toward the house with Ludlow beside him. "Were you successful in finding a building supply store that can still order windows?" he inquired.

"Most of them won't even accept orders, but I was told by a salesman that they are increasing their in-stock inventory, although they will not accept any custom-made window orders for now. Next week, they said, the windows should be in."

Ludlow had volunteered to help with purchasing, and his days were spent in procuring supplies. The sound of hammers rang out in the early morning, and the hot Florida sun was already taking the temperatures well into the eighties. The predictions were for temperatures to top one hundred degrees by afternoon. Yet the workers continued, wet with sweat and drinking gallons of water provided by the lunch van.

"This is how God meant for His family to work together," Ludlow told Millicent. "I have a greater appreciation than ever before for those who are willing to travel for hours to help others in need. Imagine, some Mennonite volunteers came all the way from Belize!"

"If we had waited for our insurance company to help, we would have been in here a long time," Millicent said, turning from the tiny refrigerator to the even tinier stove. "Mrs. Johnson told me that when they saw how quickly our house was going up, she wished they had taken the offered help instead of waiting for their agent to show up. In spite of many promises, they haven't even gotten permission to clean up their lot yet."

"The insurance companies are all overwhelmed right now," Ludlow said. "When I went to the bank yesterday, I was surprised at the coverage I got when our loan was refinanced. I know we always paid the premiums along with our payments, but if the insurance company covers us completely like the policy reads, we shouldn't incur any loss."

"Better not depend on it," Millicent said wryly. "It's a wonder there are any insurance companies still in business with all the millions of dollars they're paying out."

"Good morning," greeted Mahlon as he looked up from his desk. The mobile office was filled with paperwork.

"And a good morning it is!" Ludlow agreed with a smile.

"Sit down. Have you moved into your house?" Mahlon asked, leaning back in his office chair.

"Yes, we did," Ludlow responded jubilantly. "Praise the Lord, that house is so comfortable. This morning when we woke up and looked around, we just started praising the Lord for how good He is to us. And now our insurance check came in the mail. Our losses were fully covered." Ludlow choked up and looked through his grateful tears at Mahlon.

"That is wonderful," Mahlon said gratefully. "I praise God with you."

"I want to pay you and your people for what you have done for us. Let me know how much we owe you."

"You don't owe us anything," Mahlon replied simply. "We have done it gladly."

Ludlow shook his head. "I want to at least pay for the building materials. It would not be right to take your money and receive compensation from the insurance company as well. I insist on paying something."

Mahlon opened his ledger and scanned the pages. He entered a series of numbers on his adding machine. "I think we put about thirty thousand dollars' worth of materials in your house. If you want to contribute that amount, we will use it to help others who had no insurance."

Ludlow nodded. "How about pay for the workers?" he inquired. "Many of them took time off from their work and traveled down here. That was costly."

Mahlon held up his hand. "No, no. All the workers volunteered their time and expertise to help rebuild free of charge."

"It hardly seems fair that we should actually benefit from Hurricane Andrew," said Ludlow gratefully. "When we emerged from our destroyed home less than eight months ago, we did not dream we would be this blessed."

Mahlon nodded. "Often in the middle of a crisis, we cannot see how this devastation could ever benefit us, but afterward we see the hand of the Lord in it all."

Mahlon rose from his chair and the two men embraced before Ludlow left the little office. They were one in spirit, their hearts drawn together because of the love of Jesus Christ.

The Florida City building inspector drove up to the lot where Southmost Mennonite Church was being rebuilt. He parked his car and opened the door. Stepping out, he could hear voices coming from inside the small white tent that had been erected to shelter the worshipers until the church house could be completed.

Hurricane Andrew had leveled the church house and the small building they had used for Sunday school classes. Only the wooden pulpit had been rescued unscathed.

Paul White, the inspector, stood silently for a few minutes, listening to the prayers of the men having their morning devotions inside the tent. Then he looked at the shell of the newly constructed church house. Those volunteers were certainly doing some fast work. They had finished shingling the roof just since his visit the day before. The inspector leaned against his car and listened to the prayers. He was deep in thought.

Throughout South Florida, tens of thousands of homes had been destroyed by Hurricane Andrew, and in the aftermath of building and rebuilding, the city and county officials were kept busy day after exhausting day. Even though many more inspectors were hired to keep up with the burgeoning demand that reconstruction brought into the area, they were still kept extremely busy. Not surprisingly, many homeowners and contractors tried to take advantage of the situation by using inferior building materials or substandard construction methods.

When the men inside the tent burst into a chorus of singing, Paul reached through the open window of his car to get his clipboard. He knew the place would soon be filled with activity as the volunteers left their place of prayer. For the entire week that he had been coming here on his inspection rounds, it had always been the same.

"Mr. White!" Paul glanced at the tent and saw Ludlow coming toward him with his hand outstretched. "Good morning!" Ludlow continued. "Did you see what the boys got done yesterday?" He waved a hand toward the church building.

"Good workers," Paul said with a smile. "Of course, they're working for a good cause."

"Thank you," Ludlow responded. "God has been blessing us immensely. These people are so good to us, coming from all over the United States and even Canada to help us rebuild. How is your job going?"

Paul managed a wry grin as he said, "The usual—people trying to skimp, officials vying for positions of prestige. All the usual politics. I am exhausted most of the time." For some reason, he found it easy to talk to this tall man with the friendly smile.

Ludlow nodded sympathetically. "I see the same thing as I go for building supplies. One person is told that the supplies he needs are not available, but only minutes later I see someone else walking out with the same item. People need their lives changed by the Lord Jesus Christ."

They stood side by side and watched as the volunteer group began plastering the sides of the church. Two men were framing up the entrance porch.

"As if work isn't difficult enough, my own life is in shambles," Paul continued. "My wife left me and moved to Arizona. That was back before the hurricane, and I was going to try to forget her and make a new life. I even dated several times, but nothing ever worked out. I miss her," he added forlornly.

Ludlow wisely said nothing, but allowed Paul to pour out his feelings while he prayed silently. "I tried the whole bar thing, hoping to drown my sorrows in drink." Paul laughed bitterly. "Still do. After work, I am so tired I just head for the nearest bar and drink until I can't think anymore and then go home and sleep. It's the only way I've been able to fall asleep lately." The clipboard was still clutched in his right hand, his knuckles showing white as he gripped it tightly.

" 'Come unto me, all ye that labour and are heavy laden, and I will give you rest,' " Ludlow quoted softly. "Jesus understands the way you feel and invites you to give your life over to Him."

"I used to go to church a long time ago," Paul said reflectively. "Thought I didn't need religion anymore, though."

"You don't need religion," Ludlow agreed. "You need Jesus."

"Is there a difference?" Paul looked searchingly into Ludlow's face.

"Most of the time, yes," Ludlow responded. "Religion is a set of rules and most times is followed by those who feel they have to live a certain way to please God. To believe in Jesus is to repent from our sins and allow Him to enter our lives and take control. Then He does the cleansing and the renewing for us. We then live in obedience because we love Him, not because we're trying to make ourselves good."

"I have tried to be good, but I can't," Paul stated honestly.

Putting his hand on Paul's shoulder, Ludlow asked, "Would you want me to pray for you?"

When Paul nodded, Ludlow led him toward the tent. They knelt on the grass. Placing his hands on Paul's bowed head, Ludlow prayed for the troubled inspector. The prayer was nothing elaborate, nothing special. Ludlow talked to God and asked Him to reveal Himself to this repentant man. Even when Paul's shoulders began to shake with silent weeping, Ludlow continued to pray. He knew the Spirit was beginning to do His work in the desperate man's life.

The two remained inside the tent for thirty minutes. Paul confessed his sins to God, and when Ludlow prompted him, he asked Jesus to enter his heart and claim him for a son.

"I asked Jesus Christ to come into my heart and make me a new man," Paul White said as he stood beside the lake in the hot sunshine and shared his testimony. "I used to come to the church house every day to inspect the work while the building was under construction. I often heard the men pray in the tent. Something inside me kept telling me there was something different about these people. Not once did I feel that they resented me because I made them follow the building codes. I used to talk with Brother Ludlow and he always had time for me. I sensed that he had something I did not have. I didn't know at the time that it was Jesus." He dashed away the tears from his eyes.

The congregation from Southmost smiled in understanding and there was a murmur of agreement from the group.

"The day I spilled out my sins to Brother Ludlow was a milestone for me. I don't think I had ever told anyone what a miserable man I was. I was finally honest."

Ludlow stood silently beside his friend. He sensed the presence of God on this gathering.

"My life is still not everything I want it to be. I pray every day that my wife and I can be reunited. Brother Ludlow told me how God has healed his marriage, and I am trusting God will do the same for me. Please pray for us."

Millicent felt the pain in Paul's voice and silently cried out for Jesus to strengthen him.

"I want to be baptized because I love Jesus. He has changed my life and given me salvation for my soul. Oh, how I love Him!"

After his baptism, Paul sang heartily along with the congregation, "I will praise Him! I will praise Him! Praise the Lamb for sinners slain!" As the people clapped and sang, Paul lifted his hands and face toward heaven and gave thanks to his Saviour.

Several years later Ludlow stood in the completed church building and spread a letter out on the pulpit in front of him. "I want to read a letter from Paul to all of you," he told the congregation. "Many of you know that he moved to Arizona several months ago to live closer to his estranged wife. This is what he writes:"

Dear Brother Ludlow,

I rejoice in Jesus Christ, the living Son of God! Oh, Brother Ludlow, how I praise Him! You see, Stella and I have now been remarried for a week, and our lives are filled with awe and wonder at the great work God has done and is doing in our lives.

When I think back to that day in the tent, I feel a deep gratitude to you, brother, for the sensitivity you showed in listening to my tale of woe and in allowing the Spirit to lead you to pray for me. I want to tell you, when you laid your hands on me and prayed, something broke inside me and I felt the presence of God. When you hugged me that morning before I went to inspect the church building, it was as though God was hugging me through you. Not once did I even think about the fact that you are black and I am white. We were just one in Jesus!

I want you to thank the church there for the wonderful family they were to me during the time that I was a part of your church. With joy I remember my baptism and the many words of encouragement they gave me. Thank them for faithfully praying for the restoration of our marriage. Tell them it has happened!

Several people in the audience applauded spontaneously as Ludlow read of the restoration. Hands were raised toward the ceiling in praise as they listened closely.

While God was doing a work in my heart, He was also working in Stella's heart, but I don't think she needed to change as much as I did. Anyway, remember the time she visited in your church? She says she felt the love of God from all of you.

We have found a group of people out here in Arizona who love the Lord, and we are fellowshipping with them. The pastor who married us last week has a true heart after God.

So, once more, a big thank you! To think God used Hurricane Andrew to bring us together, and He used you to help me see that Jesus is the answer to my needs. I want to grow in Him and continue to live for Him the rest of my life.

God bless you richly, my brother, and I hope to bring my wife along the next time we come to Florida for a visit. Oh, by the way, I found a new job out here and I do not miss being a building inspector!

Yours in Christ,
Paul White

There was an outburst of praise and exclamations of joy from the congregation as Ludlow folded the letter. "What a testimony," he said with feeling. "Thank you, Lord, for rescuing Paul and restoring his marriage."

Little children, praise the Lord! Praise the Lord! Praise the Lord!
Little children, praise the Lord! Praise ye the Lord.

The group of fourteen children sang heartily, repeating the refrain over and over again. Dawn led the singing, and as they clapped and sang together, she watched the Elosiant children join in. Ketlene, the oldest at seven, had the pinched look of a girl who had grown up too early. Kendy, at five, was a happy, outgoing boy who learned quickly. Kurlin was only three and at first had wanted to run about, but as he got into the rhythm of the song, he bobbed his head and kept time with his feet.

Praise Him for our teachers dear, teachers dear . . .

Several of the older children glanced toward the church kitchen where Millicent was busy at work. They knew what would happen after the singing exercises.

The church at Southmost Mennonite had gone through many changes. When Ludlow began attending services there, he had joined as a member, but he had kept his membership at Sunnyside as well. "This will always be my church," he had told Lester Gingerich, bishop of Sunnyside. "Your mission church in Hattieville was my first spiritual family after I became a Christian."

As the years passed at Southmost, Ludlow and his family had seen a shift as a number of the Mennonite families moved north. Then Hurricane Andrew had come and destroyed the church building. After the volunteers had rebuilt it, those still attending began to be more responsive to the needs of the community around them.

The Elosiant children were among the first to come to these classes. Immigrants from Haiti, the family had been outside in their yard one day as Ludlow was on his way to church. He had not missed the opportunity to invite them to come to church with him.

"We sing and pray and teach the children Bible stories," he had told the mother. "My wife makes a breakfast for them afterward, and we invite them to stay for Sunday school."

The small crowd of children had swelled into ever larger numbers until they were divided into two groups. Dawn used her creative skills to capture and keep the children's attention as she told them about Jesus and His love for everyone.

After they had finished the last chorus of the morning song, Dawn asked, "Who knows what happens next?"

"Eat!" Kurlin said loudly. The children laughed and Dawn smiled at the little fellow's eagerness. "That's right," she chuckled. "But what do we do before that?"

"Pray," Shirley, an eight-year-old girl from the neighborhood, said quietly.

"That is right," Dawn agreed. "We pray. Does anyone have a need we should pray about?"

"I need new shoes," Tamara said, pointing to her worn and scuffed slippers.

"God don't care none about shoes. He's busy looking after the big things," Dwayne said, scoffing at the idea of praying for shoes.

"Is that true?" Dawn asked, lifting her eyebrows and looking seriously at the children. Several of them shook their heads emphatically, while others looked perplexed.

"Tell you what," Dawn said. "We are going to pray for shoes for Tamara. Then we will see if God cares about things like shoes or if He is just busy with running the world." She smiled at Dwayne. "Is that okay?"

The children looked at each other questioningly. Most of them nodded.

"Who wants to pray?" Dawn asked. "Will someone volunteer to pray for shoes for Tamara?"

"I will," Ketlene said quietly. This was the first time she had ever volunteered.

"Let's close our eyes and ask God along with Ketlene," Dawn said, setting the example.

"Now for the food that my mother has prepared," Dawn told the children as the prayer ended. They eagerly turned and went into the kitchen where the tantalizing smell of sausages had been calling them for the last twenty minutes. Many of the children stayed for Sunday school, and later, as Ludlow stood up to preach, he saw that over half of the children had chosen to stay for the entire service.

For most of them, the church family at Southmost Mennonite was an oasis of comfort and love that was sadly missing in their homes. Frequently, heart-wrenching stories of abuse, neglect, and loneliness surfaced in the Sunday morning classes.

The motivation for feeding the children was not to attract larger crowds, but to provide nourishment for children who genuinely needed the food. When the congregation realized that many of the children were malnourished, they had begun cooking breakfasts for them.

"Ha!" Junior laughed as he picked up a pair of girls' shoes from the top of the table and looked at them. "Dawn, I know you have small feet and you are as slim as ever, but there is no way your feet will fit into these." He chuckled again as he turned the sturdy shoes from side to side.

"Oh, Junior, you always have to tease me, don't you?" Dawn replied fondly. "No, I have no intentions of trying to wear these shoes. They are the answer to a little girl's prayer. Actually, they're the answer to two little girls' prayers."

Ludlow smiled as he came to join his two children. "There must be a story here," he said, grinning at Dawn.

"Yes, Daddy, there is a story. It's a story of children praying in faith and then of God moving in my heart to put shoes to the prayer." She told her family how Tamara had been willing to share her need for shoes.

"Ketlene prayed so simply, Daddy. Her prayer reminded me how we can come to God in simplicity and directness. She didn't use extra words, just spoke simply and directly. 'Lord, please send Tamara some shoes. Right now.' That was it."

"Ah," Junior said, nodding his head wisely. "So you heard from God that you were to buy shoes with your own money, and now you are the answer to a little girl's prayer."

"Something like that," Dawn said, smiling at her brother.

"Bless you, Dawn," Ludlow murmured. "I can tell the children have a special place in your heart and life. I appreciate your sacrificing personal money to help answer a child's prayer."

Dawn reached out and squeezed her father's arm affectionately. "Daddy, you know you have done the same thing over and over again. I am only following my parents' good example." She laughed as Ludlow grinned and turned away.

"Now guess what," Dawn told her class the next Sunday. "Remember last week when Tamara told us she needed shoes?" Of course they remembered. Bright eyes turned toward their teacher. They could guess from the thrill in Dawn's voice that something special was going to happen.

"Ketlene, do you remember how you prayed and asked God to bring shoes for Tamara right away?"

"He didn't do it," Ketlene retorted quickly, looking at Tamara's feet.

"Aha!" Dawn held up her hand and then reached into her big bag. She pulled out a shoe box.

"Ooh!" The children drew in their breath and stared at Dawn with wide-eyed wonder.

Ketlene's eyes grew big as Dawn placed the box into her hands. "Give this to Tamara," she instructed with a smile. "Let's see what God has done."

The shoes fit perfectly. Tamara had to put them on and walk around the classroom to the excited exclamations of her admiring classmates.

"What shall we do now that God has answered our prayers?" Dawn asked the excited children.

"Ask Him for more shoes!" Peter piped up eagerly.

Dawn laughed. "Whoa, not so fast," she said. "Let's first thank God for answering Ketlene's prayer and sending shoes for Tamara. We need to show God how thankful we are and how much we love Him for taking care of us."

This time, all the children prayed. Their prayers were simple, some merely thanking God for what He had already done for them while others prayed in faith for their family's needs. Dawn's eyes filled with tears as she listened to the children's prayers. "Except you become as a little child" came to her mind. Her own heart overflowed as she realized how God is waiting to have us all come to Him and simply trust in His goodness and providence.

The church at Southmost Mennonite was truly changing from a place where transplants from the north had met for worship to a community church where the outcasts and needy were finding a home. The Walkers threw themselves heartily into the work of the church and Ludlow was asked to serve as pastor. With the blessing of the church at Sunnyside, he accepted the call.

Many calls were still coming for him to speak in churches all over the United States and now even in other countries as well. It was with delight that Ludlow answered the call more than once to return to Belize and re-unite with his first Christian family in Hattieville. How he thanked God for those faithful people who had taken him into their hearts and loved him from the beginning of his walk with Christ. Now he was able to minister among them, and he gladly shared the Gospel in their churches.

SHIPWATCH

"Hi, my name is Ellen. Would you like a gift packet?" Even though it was after nine o'clock in the evening, the deck of the ship *Discovery* was well lit. The girl holding out the package smiled at the dark-skinned man.

"What it is?" the seaman asked, looking at the small brown envelope.

"Some little gifts for you. We want to let you know that we appreciate the cargo your ships bring to America." Ellen hoped she was doing this correctly. It had all sounded so easy during orientation with Ludlow.

The warm wind blew gently against her skirts. She glanced over at Sarah and Emma, several feet away, talking to three sailors by the rail.

"No. No need." The man shook his head but smiled at Ellen. She wondered if he thought she was selling the packet, but she didn't want to press the point. This wasn't going so well. The first man to whom she had tried to give a packet had stared at her curiously and then turned and walked away.

"Hello," a friendly voice greeted her. Ellen spun around. She saw a young man grinning at her.

"My name is Ellen. Would you like a gift packet?" she tried again, extending the package toward him.

"Oh, thank you. This is very kind of you." The young man rolled his Rs but otherwise spoke good English. "My name is Richard," he continued.

"Richard, it's nice to meet you." Ellen was relieved to find someone who finally took a packet. "Do you work on this ship?"

"Yes, for sure. I am standing on it." Richard flashed another friendly smile at her.

Ellen nodded a little sheepishly. "I guess that was a silly question. What do you do here? What is your work?" This was really working! She was getting to talk to someone and share a package.

"I do, how you say, clean the decks," Richard said, moving his arms to make mopping motions.

Ellen looked at the enormous ship deck. "All by yourself?" she asked incredulously.

Richard laughed, "Yes. I have days and days to do this. Even weeks."

By this time he had opened the package. "Toothbrush. That is needed. Ah, toothpaste. Thank you very much." He lifted the bar of soap to his nose and breathed in deeply. "Ah, it is smelling good," he laughed pleasantly. Then he found the Gospel tract. His eyes lit up and he read aloud, "'How to Know if You Are Saved.' Yes, this is good." His voice was animated. "Yes, I am believer in Jesus Christ!" He lifted the booklet to his lips.

"You are a believer?" he asked Ellen.

"Oh, yes," Ellen assured him. "Yes, I am a Christian."

"This is wonderful. To meet a person who is Christian is very encouraging. Other packets have papers in them too?" He looked at the other young people who were talking with the ship workers on the deck.

"Yes, they all have them."

"Oh, may I have one more for my friend Dimitrios? He need to read this because I think he not a Christian."

Ellen took another packet out of her bag. "Here, this is for your friend," she told him.

Richard took it and smiled gratefully. "This is a good day," he said.

Ludlow came up to where the two were chatting. "Hello, my name is Ludlow," he said, reaching out and shaking Richard's hand warmly.

"My name is Richard Urbonas. I am from Lithuania. I have here your paper about Jesus. I am a believer too."

"That's wonderful," Ludlow rejoiced. "We have included information in the packet about our correspondence Bible study course. If you are interested, fill out the form and mail it to us or give it to us before we leave and we will send you our Bible study courses," Ludlow told the young man.

"It is from the Bible, this course?" Richard asked.

"It sure is," Ludlow assured him. "It is a teaching from the Gospel of John. Ten lessons."

"Oh, I want," Richard told them enthusiastically.

The dining hall where the ship's crew ate was nothing fancy, but as Ludlow and the volunteers who had joined him for Shipwatch sat down for a nighttime meal at 10:30, the room was filled with friendly chatter.

"Oh, yes, the crew always wants us to eat with them," Ludlow had told them earlier. "It gives us an opportunity to talk with them, and sometimes they have a lot of questions about spiritual things. I use every opportunity to tell the crew about Jesus."

"How long have you been doing this?" Brian, one of the young men who had volunteered, asked.

"I started Shipwatch in 1990. This is 1999, so I guess that makes nine years," Ludlow told them.

"What made you think about this ministry?" Ellen asked.

"I was moved by God to witness to unreached people, and I remembered my years on cargo ships when I was a young man. So I inquired here at the port," Ludlow began. "Since I had been a ship's officer and knew my way around ports and aboard ships, it was easy for me to get to know the right people. God continued to open the doors, and I began the Agape Christian Ministries for doing the Bible courses. My wife helps me with the correspondence courses, and we get letters all the time from people asking for advice and prayers."

"I talked with a Barbara from Poland," Annette, another volunteer, told the group. "She has been working on ships for five years, traveling all over the world."

"I was amazed at the number of nationalities on board one ship," Brian said, shaking his head. "There were workers from Greece, Guatemala,

India, and the Philippines. And they all spoke English. Kind of," he added with a laugh.

"English is the common language, but I try to make sure I have tracts in their own language too," Ludlow said. "It means so much to them to receive literature in their native language, but yes, most of them can speak and read English. It is a requirement on most of the ships."

The group had a time of prayer before leaving the ship around midnight. When they took count, they found that they had given out about twenty-five gift packets, all with Gospel literature tucked inside along with the toiletries.

The young man on the pier walked toward Ludlow. His close-cropped black hair and well-fitting clothes showed attention to detail. There was an air of confidence in his steps, and as the two men approached each other, they made eye contact.

"Good morning," Ludlow said with a friendly nod. "Are you on shore leave?"

"Yes, sir," came the courteous answer. Then with a wave of his hand toward the cruise ship tied up along the pier, the young man said with pride, "*Splendor of the Seas.*"

"Nice," Ludlow said, taking in the enormous hulk of the docked ship. The young man smiled broadly and his white teeth flashed friendliness in his dark face. He reached out his hand, saying, "I'm Sheldon Glasglow."

Ludlow took the proffered hand and shook it warmly. "Ludlow Walker. Here is a small gift for you."

Sheldon took the package. "Ah, thank you, sir. I always need toiletries."

"Sheldon, are you a Christian?" Ludlow asked kindly. "Do you know Jesus Christ?"

For a moment Sheldon dropped his gaze, and then looking squarely into Ludlow's eyes he said, "I'm not a practicing Christian. I used to go to church and all that. With Mama. But then I got this job and—well," he shrugged his shoulders, "I just kind of quit. Thought I outgrew it, I guess."

Sending a silent prayer to God, Ludlow asked simply, "Sheldon, have you ever been born again?"

"What's that?" the young man inquired sincerely.

"Hey, if you have some time, let's sit down on this bench. I would love to explain to you what being born again means," Ludlow told him eagerly.

The morning sun began to bake South Florida with heat, but the two men on the bench were oblivious to the temperature and humidity. "And that's what it means to be born again," Ludlow told the young man after explaining the way of salvation. "Repenting from your sins and asking the Lord Jesus Christ to enter your heart and life and make you clean. He will forgive you for all your sins and give you power to live for Him."

Sheldon studied his fingers splayed on his knee.

"You can do it right here, right now," Ludlow told him. He sensed the Spirit was calling his new friend.

"Right here? On the pier?" Sheldon looked around him and then up at Ludlow.

"If you want to, yes. God hears us wherever we are. He is looking for a soft and repentant heart. Give your life to Jesus. He is waiting, and He will respond," Ludlow urged.

"Are you sure?" Sheldon asked bluntly.

Ludlow nodded confidently. "He heard me when I cried out to Him. He can hear you too. We can pray right here. Okay?"

Sheldon bowed his head and then he nodded. He wiped his nose with the back of his hand.

"Yes, Jesus," Ludlow said without any formality. "You are here, listening to us talk to you. You see this young man and you know his heart. Listen to his cries, Lord, and meet with him by the power of the Holy Spirit." Ludlow paused and waited.

Sheldon's eyes began to fill with tears. "I don't know how to pray," he said in a broken voice. "I don't even know if God will hear me. I have sinned so many times."

"Tell the Lord all about it just like you told me. You told me you have sinned. Now tell God all about it."

At first the words were hesitant, like a toddler's first steps. Then Sheldon began confessing sins, and through his tears he asked God to forgive him. Ludlow prayed along with his friend.

The two sat side by side on the bench, and as the Spirit moved into the young man's life, there was a sudden note of joy in his voice. "Thank you, Jesus!" he exclaimed. "Something is different inside. I feel clean and, well, lighter. Some kind of weight is gone from my heart." Sheldon put his hand on his chest.

Ludlow laughed and placed his hand on Sheldon's shoulder. "That is a good way of wording it. Jesus lifts our burdens and makes us clean inside. Here is a copy of the Gospel of John, Sheldon." Ludlow took a paperback booklet out of his bag. "Read it every day and ask God to help you understand what you read."

Sheldon nodded and opened it.

"I will give you a packet of tracts as well. You can share them with the other workers. Tell people what happened to you. God wants you to share your testimony with others. It will strengthen you and it will be a testimony for Jesus."

"Peggy! I'll tell Peggy," Sheldon told Ludlow with a broad smile. "My girlfriend," he explained.

"Is she on the ship?" Ludlow asked.

Shaking his head, Sheldon explained. "We met on the ship. She was a passenger, and in my work as a dining room steward, we got to know each other. It just went on from there. We fell in love."

Two pigeons flew in with a flurry of feathers and strutted on the pavement. Sheldon watched them thoughtfully. "We spent a lot of time together. When she got off the ship in California, I lived with her while I was on shore leave. She told me I could come see her anytime."

One of the pigeons cocked its head sideways and looked at the two men inquiringly. A sudden wave of Sheldon's arms sent the two birds fleeing into the sunshine. "I lived with her and we are not married," Sheldon said with pain in his voice. "Is that a sin I need to repent of too?"

"What do you think?" Ludlow asked, wanting the conviction to come from the Spirit rather than himself.

"God doesn't like it," Sheldon said simply. "Deep down inside, I knew what we were doing was not right. My mama did not like it, but I didn't care."

Ludlow nodded and smiled in satisfaction as the newborn Christian lifted his face toward heaven, confessing his sin and receiving the forgiveness of God.

Dear Pastor Walker,

Greetings in the most wonderful name of the Lord. I do hope by the blessing of God that this letter meets you and your family in the best of health. I want to say thank you for everything that you have done and are doing for me in getting me a better knowledge and understanding of God's Word.

I received the reply from my first Bible lesson and was very glad. I even started showing it to everyone on board and now I have another member for your outreach. His name is Bertie, and if it pleases you, I want you to send him a Bible correspondence course. The address is the same as mine, but his position is cabin attendant.

Pastor, I even started a Bible class on the ship. On the first night not many were in attendance because another group was having a party on the ship, and you know that men love the pleasures of this world rather than God. However, I am praying that God will send more folks the next time. I am trying to do this every Sunday night as God permits me. I want the church to pray for me as I try to share the Word of God on the ocean.

I am now sending the next lesson for you to grade. If you want to send me two or three in one letter, no problem. I can just do them and send them back to you.

So until I hear from you again, may God bless you and your family, including your church family, as you endeavor to do His work. May He open doors for you as you teach His Word. Pray for me as I do the same for you. May God bless us all in Jesus' name, Amen.

Always,
Sheldon Glasglow

Ludlow leaned back in his desk chair and stared at the letter. "Thank you, Lord!" A smile spread over his face and his thoughts went back to the time when he had first met Sheldon. In his first letter after his conversion, Sheldon had requested to begin the "Studies in the Gospel According to John." Ludlow had gladly enrolled him and the completed tests began to show up shortly afterward.

It was obvious that God was doing a wonderful work in the young man's life. He went through the course rapidly and was almost finished. So eager was he for material that, as he had just written, he wanted several lessons in one packet.

"I wrote to Peggy and told her that I am now a follower of Jesus. I told her that I would no longer stay with her overnight and I was sorry for my sins." Ludlow remembered these lines from a letter he had received earlier. He had been thrilled with the spiritual growth in Sheldon. When he had received the letter concerning Peggy, he had known that this young man was serious about his walk with God.

Dear Pastor Walker,

Greetings in the name of Jesus! He is a wonderful Saviour. I am so excited to write to you that Peggy wants to enroll in your Bible correspondence course. She is going to church with her mother, and when I wrote to her about my becoming a Christian, she wrote me a long letter, telling me that she knew what she had been doing was wrong and that she also wants to live for Jesus!

This is good news for me. I was willing to forget all about her, but now Jesus is changing her life too. I will give her address to you, and could you please send her the first lesson?

My job on the ship is going well and I am continuing my Bible study class. One young man gave his life to Jesus and others are repenting. We have very good times together and we encourage each other in the Lord.

I hope to see you the next time we get to Miami. May God bless you very richly with His favor on your life and on your family's life.

Respectfully,
Sheldon Glasglow

"Over here, Pastor Walker!"

Ludlow turned, and there in the airport was a radiant Sheldon, guiding a young woman by the elbow. "Peggy, this is Pastor Ludlow Walker. Ludlow, my fiancé Peggy." Sheldon's eyes beamed with joy as he introduced the two.

Ludlow greeted Peggy heartily, "I am so glad to meet you!"

"And I am delighted to meet you. Sheldon has talked so much about you that I felt I already knew you," Peggy replied. She smiled up at the minister.

"It means so much to us that you have come to our wedding," Sheldon said heartily. "Peggy has such a big family and so many friends here in Oakland, but my family is all back in Africa. So, Pastor Walker, you will represent my family! You are my spiritual papa!"

The three laughed joyously together as they went to collect Ludlow's luggage in the baggage claim area.

When the invitation had arrived to attend Sheldon's wedding in Oakland, California, Ludlow had made immediate plans to attend. There had never been any doubt in his mind that he wanted to bless the young couple who had become a part of his life through letters and the Bible correspondence course. His heart overflowed with gratitude to God at the realization that these precious lives had been plucked from the enemy's hands and would be a strong force for the glory of God's kingdom.

CHAPTER 24

INTO ALL THE WORLD

"Welcome, Pastor! Welcome!" Ludlow got out of the Jeep in which he had been traveling the rough India roads with Alvin Miller and returned the smiling welcome of the group of men coming to meet them.

"We welcome you to our humble village in the name of Jesus," Jakob Prakashan said, reaching out with both hands to grasp Ludlow's hands. He bent forward and kissed Ludlow on each cheek.

Bowing and smiling, several other men came forward with flower garlands and placed them around the necks of the two visitors. Ludlow's heart warmed immediately, and in spite of the fatigue of the long journey, his spirit was refreshed by the loving and heartfelt joy the brothers showed to them.

"You are tired," Jakob said, steering them toward his house. "Maresha has prepared some tea." Groups of onlookers in the street watched the arrival of the guests with interest.

Ludlow followed his host gratefully. Previous visits had always followed the same routine—a time of refreshment and blissful rest before being thrown into a whirlwind of activities.

The village of Bouwal was small, but Ludlow and Alvin were amazed at the number of people who thronged the village as well as the cities through which they had traveled.

"Welcome to our home in the name of Jesus," Maresha said in English as her husband ushered the two into their comfortable house. She pushed two stools forward as Ludlow and Alvin slipped off their shoes and stepped onto the rug before taking their seats on the backless chairs. Jakob and Maresha were thoughtful enough to make sure that any visitors from the West had stools to sit on, rather than obliging their guests to sit cross-legged on the floor as they themselves did.

The tea was hot and spicy and the small cookies that were sprinkled with anise seeds were not very sweet. In spite of the unfamiliar flavors, the two men gratefully munched the refreshing snack.

"You must rest," Jakob told them. "Come, I will show you to your rooms."

"You are so kind," Ludlow told his hosts. "The first flight from Miami was an overnight flight, and by the time we got to Frankfurt, I was already tired. I spent most of the next flight to Bombay trying to sleep in my seat."

Alvin laughed. "The sight of Ludlow trying to fit his tall frame into a comfortable position on the airplane was quite interesting." Their hosts joined in the laughter as they imagined the scene.

"Then you still had the next flight to Hyderabad and the two-hour trip to our house by Jeep," Jakob said. "Yes, yes, you must be tired. Come and rest."

The guests gratefully followed their host upstairs to a cool room where a mattress, complete with sheets and pillows, lay on the floor.

"Ah, what pleasure just to stretch out completely," Ludlow sighed, breathing deeply and dropping his head on a pillow.

"Water! Water!" The excited cry went up from the group of onlookers as the well drillers stepped back from the newly dug well.

Ludlow and Alvin were among the group. Pastor Jakob had told them about the excitement that was building in a neighboring village among the residents when the well drillers had arrived.

"This has been one of the most effective ways to preach the Gospel of Jesus," Jakob had told his guests. "When they see the wells right in their own villages and they are told that Christians from around the world are paying for this, they are overwhelmed and want to hear why foreigners would do this for them."

Ludlow nodded as he looked at the excited villagers thronging around the well. "Where did they get their water before the well was here?" he asked.

With a wave of his hand toward the river, Jakob replied, "From there."

Ludlow and Alvin looked toward the river. A short distance upstream, women were scrubbing their laundry. Farther on, a small tributary flowed into the brown waters, leaving a grey streak all along the bank as sewage floated on the surface.

"Yes," Jakob said. "They are always extremely grateful. We tell them that Jesus changes the hearts of His people, and they want to share His kindness with others. We conduct meetings after the wells are dug and most of the people want to attend."

"Praise the Lord!" Ludlow was touched by the way the gift of water opened doors to share the Water of Life.

The clicking sounds of busy fingers on keyboards filled the crowded and somewhat stuffy room where more than twenty boys sat in front of their computers. Alvin and Ludlow watched with interest from the doorway. Sure, the computers were old and slow, and the boys often had to wait while the screens loaded, but the diligent students exuded an air of excitement.

"They know that if they master computer skills, they will have much better opportunities for employment, and that is what drives them on in spite of outdated equipment," Jakob's son, Sam, told them.

"How long do they stay and study?" Alvin asked.

"Sometimes until we drive them out," Sam said with a smile. "There is very little else they want to do, for this can be an opportunity for a better life."

"My name is Steven. I am glad to meet you." The speaker was a young man perhaps in his early twenties. His words were carefully articulated but almost void of expression as he struggled to speak English.

"And we are glad to meet you," Ludlow echoed pleasantly. "How long have you been studying here?"

Steven fastened his eyes on Ludlow's face and smiled, but did not answer. Sam quickly translated the question for him, and then Steven nodded. "I have studied nine month," he said mechanically.

"Good. You are learning English well," Alvin told him encouragingly. Steven nodded and smiled and returned to his keyboard.

"Learning English as a second language will increase their chances of employment by 500 percent," Sam explained. "Even gaining extensive computer skills won't be of much value unless they become proficient in speaking and understanding English."

"He did speak English quite well," Ludlow observed, "but he had a hard time understanding any questions."

"That is very common," Sam replied. "They study and memorize many words and then advance to proper usage and grammar. But when they actually hear native English speakers like you, it makes no sense to them because they are not used to your inflections."

As they stood and watched the lit screens and the flying fingers on the keyboards, Alvin said reflectively, "Maybe I will have more patience with the technical support people when I call for help with my computer system. Sometimes I get frustrated by the difficulties they have in understanding me when I explain my problem."

Ludlow nodded in agreement. "When it means a tenfold increase in their income, they will indeed try to get into positions where they can learn even more."

Ludlow stood in front of the congregation on a Sunday morning during the second and final week of their visit. "It is always a privilege for me to come and see what God through the Holy Spirit is doing in your village," he said with a smile, his hand resting on his open Bible.

Pastor Jakob fluently interpreted his words into the local dialect. The crowd nodded and murmurs of welcome rose up from the people sitting on the mats inside the simple church building.

"I want to encourage you in your faith and in your love for Jesus," Ludlow continued.

Led by a young man, the hour of worship had been an inspiration to Ludlow, even if the melodies were strange to his ears and the words completely incomprehensible. Yet as the men and women and youth had worshiped enthusiastically and fervently, sometimes with tears, he had been deeply moved. These people expressed their love for Jesus without reservation.

"Jesus went to the cross and gave His life for us so we could have eternal life." In the pause while Jakob translated, Ludlow looked at the orderly group of people in front of him. The men sat on the left side, the women on the right; all were dressed in traditional Indian clothes. Several rows of children were in the front, all eagerly listening to his words.

"When Jesus cried out, 'My God, my God, why hast thou forsaken me?' He voluntarily separated Himself from God for a time," Ludlow continued. People nodded and several lifted their hands heavenward as the words came to them through Jakob.

"Jesus did this so that we never, ever have to be separated from Him when we become Christians." Like thirsty soil, the listeners eagerly took in the message as the rain from heaven poured into their lives. "One of the most precious truths that has ever been given to me is that no matter what happens, I never have to be separated from the presence of God, who lives inside my heart."

Jakob had begun interpreting before Ludlow had completely finished his sentence, and there was a wave of subdued sound as the congregation spontaneously praised God for that truth. Ludlow was deeply moved himself. These people had such a simple faith in God. Their hearts were tender, and when they received Bible teaching, they were eager to embrace it.

Ludlow continued speaking. He knew that the services could easily last four hours or more because of the hunger and eagerness for more Bible teaching. He knew the extended service was not only because visitors were with them. Jakob often spoke of meetings that continued the entire day as the people opened themselves in worship and prayer.

They certainly knew how to pray. It had been evident just this morning as the people's voices had been lifted up in praise and prayer for over half an hour while the children had been in their Sunday school classes.

"My dear people, I feel as though you should be teaching me," Ludlow continued. "I am so blessed every time I come and see your sincere desire to follow the Lord." It was true. As eager as Pastor Jakob and the congregation always were in receiving visitors, their own sincerity and devotion never failed to encourage Ludlow greatly. "I am so privileged to be your brother in Jesus and to come to visit you," he told them sincerely.

As the service progressed, it almost seemed that time stood still as the people in the humble Indian village pressed forward in their hearts to know and understand the way of God better.

Eventually the singing started anew and a deacon came forward holding a cup in his hand. No one needed to interpret for the visitors as the congregation came forward to receive communion. As the singing rose heavenward in praise to Jesus for His sacrifice and for the joy He gave them, no translation was needed. The Spirit communicated the fervor of the worshipers, and it echoed in the visitors' own hearts.

"Let me tell you about a service we had just recently," Jakob told the two men on the last evening of their visit. "God was there with us in truth."

"Yes," Alvin said with interest, "we want to hear it." Both he and Ludlow were all ears.

"It was after a dream was given to me by God. And it was connected to a message you preached the last time you were here," he told Ludlow.

Ludlow furrowed his brow. What had he preached about the last time? It must have been at least three years ago.

"Feet washing," Jakob said with a smile, jogging Ludlow's memory.

"Oh, yes. I remember now."

Jakob began his story:

"Wash the feet of the brothers. Maresha is to wash the feet of the sisters." Not only did I distinctly hear the voice in my dream, but I saw the heavenly messenger speaking to me. When I woke up, the message in the dream was echoing in my mind.

It was still dark outside in the Indian night. Beside me, my wife lay sleeping. "It is a sign of humility and of your willingness to be a servant. God calls us to be servants to each other, in love serving the needs of our brothers and sisters. Feet washing services are a beautiful way of expressing this desire to be servants." I could almost hear Brother Ludlow Walker's voice as he had spoken about feet washing to the congregation.

I had taken the teaching to heart and brought it before the Lord. "God, you show me if you want us to practice this strange custom from the Mennonites." My prayer had been sincere, and I had studied the Bible diligently. My heart had beat with joy as I discovered that this was not merely a Mennonite custom, but an example set by Jesus Himself as He washed His disciples' feet.

"Oh, Jesus, I wish I could have washed your feet!" I had prayed sincerely. Now the dream had confirmed it. There was no doubt that God had given me His answer. We were to wash feet in humble service to one another.

"This morning, before we go to our homes, God wants me to do something for you," I said to the congregation. "Do you remember when Brother Ludlow was here and talked about washing feet?"

Heads nodded and an air of expectancy swept over the seated people.

"I prayed about it and studied the Bible and told the Lord that I am willing to obey. This week He spoke to me in a dream and told me to wash your feet."

"Ah!" the congregation exclaimed softly, eager but slightly apprehensive at the same time.

"I will wash the feet of the men and my wife will wash the feet of the women," I continued. Several of the women giggled nervously and the children laughed aloud. Washing feet in church? This was a novel experience!

I poured water into a tin basin. I approached the first man, and since the brother was already barefooted, it was an easy thing to take the washcloth and wash the man's feet. One by one, I went to all the men and boys and knelt before them, washing their feet, while Maresha did the same for the women.

Someone began singing softly, and a sense of the beauty and solemnity of the occasion swept over the church. Unexpectedly, one of the men got up and approached me. "I want to wash your feet," he told me with a smile. "I want the blessing from God on my life and I want to serve you as you have served me."

"Sure," I said, delighted by the believers' willingness to embrace this new truth. The service continued as more and more people began approaching each other and offering to wash one another's feet. Eventually more than a hundred and fifty people participated in our first feet-washing service as we took to heart one of God's beautiful ways to show our love and humility and service to each other.

As Jakob's story ended, Ludlow and Alvin sat silently, taking in the impact of what had happened. "God bless you, Jakob, for your willingness to be obedient to the voice of the Spirit," Ludlow said, reaching out and grasping the hand of his friend.

"He has blessed me, and may the Lord bless you for your faithfulness in speaking to us about this wonderful privilege of sharing with each other our love for Jesus," Jakob replied simply. "I know that God has used this service to heal hurts among us and to make our love for each other and for Jesus grow deeper and more solid."

CHAPTER 25

CHURCH AT WORK

"I want to especially praise God for His goodness to me," Ali told the group of worshipers at Southmost Mennonite Church one morning. "I am finding His presence sweet every day." The congregation listened carefully. Whenever Ali had something to share, it was sure to be an encouragement to everyone.

"Ever since I gave my life to the Lord Jesus Christ here six years ago, I am continually amazed that His love is so intense, so real in my life," Ali spoke earnestly.

Ludlow listened and marveled again at how God had changed this former Muslim man. He had been invited by Manny, the associate pastor, to attend their services. One Sunday he had stood and confessed his desire to become a Christian.

"I have this burning fire inside me that wants to tell all the lost about the Saviour," Ali now continued. "I know the more I feel the love of Jesus in my life, the more I have this . . . this fountain bubbling out from deep inside me."

The people nodded. They could identify with this small, dark, intense man from Trinidad. He had become such a part of the congregation that it was hard to remember a time when he had not been among the eager worshipers.

"I will not let the stuff of this world, the pressures of daily living, or the lures of Satan detract me from what Jesus has in store for me, both here on earth or in the future in heaven." This testimony was all the more remarkable coming from a man whose wife was steadfast in her own Hindu religion, spurning the idea that the God of the Western world could ever mean anything to her.

"If you people would, please pray for the souls who are getting the tracts in the mall. I pray that the Holy Spirit would open their hearts and the light of Jesus would shine in," Ali concluded.

"Come, let's gather around our brother and pray," Ludlow said, stepping out from behind the pulpit. Several others joined him in prayer for Ali.

Everyone knew Ali's story and the difficulty his activities had caused for him in his job at the auto parts store.

"You must stop distributing tracts at the shopping centers and the mall," Ali's boss had told him. "We are getting complaints from people who are shopping there. They see our company logo on your uniform and call us to protest."

Ali had a quick solution. "All right, I will change into my regular clothes during my lunch break. I must do what God has put on my heart to do." His boss scowled but said nothing more.

For the past five and a half years Ali had used his hour-long lunch break almost every day to distribute thousands of tracts among the crowds of shoppers in South Florida. Then had come another test. "Mall policy does not allow you to spread religious propaganda," the security officer had told him after months of his faithful mission.

Ali was ready to meet this challenge as well. "I see others distributing political material and sale flyers. I simply ask for the same leniency you give them."

Perhaps it was Ali's gentle demeanor and straightforward, simple answers that moved the security personnel. In any case, there was no more harassment. One officer even told Ali that there was an agreement among the security personnel to not push the issue, even after shoppers complained to them about the zealous man's efforts.

As they prayed for Ali, Ludlow was moved to think of this man's unswerving dedication to the mission God had given him. "Lord, bless

Ali and continue to let him feel your presence constantly in his life."

After church, even though there was a fellowship meal, Ali slipped away. They all knew that his wife insisted that he not linger and talk with the believers but come home to her immediately. He respected her wishes and continued to love her the best he knew how, hoping she would come to love and serve the God he so faithfully served.

"Pastor Ludlow! Pastor Ludlow!" Ludlow turned toward the voice. The supermarket was crowded with faces and he did not immediately recognize any of them. Then a young woman separated herself from the shoppers and hurried toward him. "Pastor Ludlow! It is so good to see you!" The young lady reached out and shook his hand warmly. "The Lord must have wanted us to meet here."

Ludlow pushed his shopping cart to one side and looked at her intently. She looked familiar, but he could not place her in his memory. "Vanessa!" she exclaimed, seeing Ludlow's confusion. "Don't you remember me? Vanessa Thanson, from Agape Women's Home."

Suddenly his memory returned, and with a wide smile Ludlow said, "Vanessa! Yes, of course, I do remember you."

Grinning, Vanessa asked, "How could you ever forget the woman who was so distraught that one Sunday morning? Do you remember how I was so ashamed of myself for weeping and I couldn't stop? I didn't know at the time that Jesus was breaking my heart so He could heal it."

Ludlow nodded. "Yes, I remember. And I remember when you did the Bible courses, your eagerness to learn kept us busy checking your test sheets. And your testimony of deliverance from drugs and addictions astonished and blessed many. How are you doing now?"

They stepped back and waited as a mother with a wailing baby in her cart pushed around them. "I have found a church where the pastor loves the Lord intently. When I was offered a job north of Miami, I wondered what would happen to me and if I would remain faithful to my Jesus, but He was so good in letting me find Calvary Chapel. I still have my job."

"And your love for the Lord, is it growing?" Ludlow knew how difficult it was for many to survive once they left programs and support staff.

"I confess I don't always put Jesus first in my life, but He is always so merciful in bringing me back to Him." Then spying someone coming into their aisle, Vanessa called out with an eager wave of her hand, "Elsie, come here! I want you to meet the man who was the teacher at the rehab. He's the one who helped me become a Christian."

A pleasant, middle-aged woman came to meet them with a smile. "Glad to meet you, sir," she said, shaking hands with Ludlow.

"Elsie is a constant comfort to me. She is my sister in the Lord and my mentor. When I am stumped with questions or don't know what to do in work situations, she is the one who prays with me and gives me advice. She is my first-rate companion." Vanessa lovingly patted Elsie's shoulder.

"Oh, Vanessa, you don't know how often your faith has strengthened mine," Elsie said with a laugh.

"This is wonderful," Ludlow said sincerely. "Meeting you, Vanessa, and hearing your testimony and knowing that God has brought other believers into your life is very encouraging. You are a living testimony that Jesus can and does change people by the power of His strength in us."

After chatting for several more minutes in the supermarket, Ludlow prayed with the two women. It was wonderful to see lives bearing fruit from the seeds that had been sown years earlier.

"But I have been a Christian for years," George said with a slight frown. "When Millicent asked if I knew Jesus, I said yes, because as a child I had responded and was baptized."

Ludlow waited. This man was sincere, and when he had asked to speak to Ludlow after the prayer service, Ludlow had sensed something was troubling the newcomer.

The Tuesday morning prayer clinic was a time for the men of the community to come together and share in prayer before beginning their day's work. George had come eagerly after Ludlow had invited him.

"I have no power," George told Ludlow. "There are things in my life that I know are sin, but I try to stop and I can't. It's like Satan has me in his grip."

"Have you ever repented from your sins? Have you ever invited Jesus into your heart? Has the Holy Spirit filled you with Christ?" Ludlow sensed that perhaps George did not understand what salvation through faith really was.

"I don't know," George said honestly, "but I want to have Jesus. I need power."

"The thief on the cross cried out to Jesus for help," Ludlow reminded him. "George, if you cry out to Jesus, He will help you. He will save you."

Patiently, lovingly, Ludlow guided the man to an understanding of God's great provision for mankind. Step by step he took him through the verses in the Bible that pointed out God's plan of salvation.

George listened closely. He nodded his head, showing his understanding. Finally he began confessing his sins and calling on God to make him a new person. When they finally rose from their knees, Ludlow embraced George. "I am so free! Thank you, Jesus!" George said, taking a deep breath. "I feel different inside. I'm clean!"

As Ludlow drove home later, he prayed softly, "This is one more piece of evidence that the time we spend in reaching people for you, Lord, is not in vain. We meet for a long time without many results, and the attendance at the prayer clinic builds and wanes, but times like these make it all worthwhile. Help me never to grow weary in well doing, Lord."

EPILOGUE

Brother Ludlow still travels extensively, speaking to people everywhere about what God has done for him. Whether in the United States or in other countries of the world, his primary desire is to tell people about the saving grace of Jesus Christ. He also hopes that Christians will be encouraged by his testimony and will learn from his experiences, whether it be a warning from his godless life or a challenge from his complete surrender to God and to the work He called Ludlow to do.

Ludlow distributes Christian literature in Shipwatch.

Ludlow is not seeking recognition for himself, but is humbled to know that God has chosen him to be a messenger of the Gospel. He continues to work with Shipwatch, to pastor his church, and to write and publish a quarterly newsletter.

Dawn and Ludlow Junior have both moved on to homes of their own, but Millicent continues to assist Ludlow in his work. Their story is not over. God continues to bless Ludlow with divine inspiration, and even though he is in his seventies, it is evident that he continues to learn at the feet of Jesus.

My wife and I feel deeply privileged to have met the Walker family, and their lives continue to inspire us, as they have so many others.

—Harvey Yoder
October 2009

ABOUT THE AUTHOR

Harvey Yoder and his wife Karen live in the beautiful mountains of western North Carolina. They have five children, all of whom are married, as well as seven grandchildren. A teacher for many years, Harvey is now a licensed real estate agent in addition to being a prolific writer. He has traveled extensively while gathering materials for his many books, most of which have been published by Christian Aid Ministries. Harvey finds it especially fulfilling to write the inspiring accounts of faithful believers whose stories would otherwise remain unknown. His greatest desire in writing is that his readers will not merely be entertained by the stories, but rather be motivated to seek God with all their hearts.

Harvey enjoys hearing from readers and can be contacted by e-mail at harveYoder@juno.com or written in care of Christian Aid Ministries, P.O. Box 360, Berlin, Ohio, 44610.

CHRISTIAN AID MINISTRIES

Christian Aid Ministries (CAM) was founded in 1981 as a nonprofit, tax-exempt, 501(c)(3) organization. Our primary purpose is to provide a trustworthy, efficient channel for Amish, Mennonite, and other conservative Anabaptist groups and individuals to minister to physical and spiritual needs around the world.

Annually, CAM distributes approximately fifteen million pounds of food, clothing, medicines, seeds, Bibles, Bible story books, and other Christian literature. Most of the aid goes to needy children, orphans, and Christian families. The main purposes of giving material aid are to help and encourage God's people and to bring the Gospel to a lost and dying world.

CAM's home office is in Berlin, Ohio. In Ephrata, Pennsylvania, CAM has a 55,000 square feet distribution center where food parcels are packed and other relief shipments organized. Next to the distribution center is our meat canning facility. CAM is also associated with seven clothing centers—located in Indiana, Iowa, Illinois, Maryland, Pennsylvania, West Virginia, and Ontario, Canada—where clothing, footwear, comforters, and fabric are received, sorted, and prepared for shipment overseas.

CAM has staff, bases, and distribution networks in Romania, Moldova, Ukraine, Haiti, Nicaragua, Liberia, and Israel. Through our International Crisis (IC) program we also help victims of famine, war, and natural disasters throughout the world. In the USA, volunteers organized under our Disaster Response Services (DRS) program help rebuild in low-income communities devastated by natural disasters such as floods, tornados, and hurricanes. We operate medical clinics in Haiti and Nicaragua.

CAM is controlled by a ten-member board of directors and operated by a five-member executive committee. The organizational structure includes an audit review committee, executive council, ministerial committee, several support committees, and department managers.

CAM is largely a volunteer organization aside from management, supervisory personnel, and bookkeeping operations. Each year, volunteers at our warehouses, field bases, and on Disaster Response Services and International Crisis projects donate more than 200,000 hours.

CAM issues an annual, audited financial statement to its entire mailing list (statements are also available upon request). Fundraising and non-aid administrative expenses are kept as low as possible. Usually these expenses are about one percent of income, which includes cash and donated items in kind.

CAM's ultimate goal is to glorify God and enlarge His kingdom. ". . . whatsoever ye do, do all to the glory of God." (1 Corinthians 10:31)

For more information or to sign up for CAM's monthly newsletter, please write or call:

Christian Aid Ministries
P.O. Box 360
Berlin, OH 44610
Phone: 330.893.2428
Fax: 330.893.2305

ADDITIONAL BOOKS

PUBLISHED BY CHRISTIAN AID MINISTRIES

God Knows My Size! / *by Harvey Yoder*
How God answered Silvia Tarniceriu's specific prayer
251 pages $10.99

They Would Not Be Silent / *by Harvey Yoder*
Testimonies of persecuted Christians in Eastern Europe
231 pages $10.99

They Would Not Be Moved / *by Harvey Yoder*
More testimonies of Christians who stood strong under communism
208 pages $10.99

Elena—Strengthened Through Trials / *by Harvey Yoder*
A young Romanian girl strengthened through hardships
240 pages $10.99

Where Little Ones Cry / *by Harvey Yoder*
The sad trails of abandoned children in Liberia during civil war
168 pages plus 16-page picture section $10.99

Wang Ping's Sacrifice / *by Harvey Yoder*
Vividly portrays the house church in China
191 pages $10.99

A Small Price to Pay / *by Harvey Yoder*
Mikhail Khorev's story of suffering under communism
247 pages $10.99

Tsunami!—*from a few that survived* / *by Harvey Yoder*
Survivors tell their stories, some with sorrow and heartbreak, others
with joy and hope.
168 pages $11.99

Tears of the Rain / *by Ruth Ann Stelfox*
Poignantly honest account of a missionary family in war-torn Liberia
479 pages $13.99

A Greater Call / *by Harvey Yoder*
What will it cost Wei to spread the Gospel in China?
195 pages $11.99

Angels in the Night / *by Pablo Yoder*
Pablo Yoder family's experiences in Waslala, Nicaragua
356 pages $12.99

The Happening / *by Harvey Yoder*
Nickel Mines school shooting—healing and forgiveness
173 pages $11.99

In Search of Home / *by Harvey Yoder*
The true story of a Muslim family's miraculous conversion
240 pages $11.99

HeartBridge / *by Johnny Miller*
Joys and sorrows at the Nathaniel Christian Orphanage
272 pages $12.99

The Long Road Home / *by Pablo Yoder*
Will prayers and the Spirit's promptings bring young Pablo "home"?
456 pages $12.99

Miss Nancy / *by Harvey Yoder*
The fascinating story of God's work through the life of an Amish
missionary in Belize
273 pages $11.99

Into Their Hands / *by Harvey Yoder*
Bible smugglers find ingenious ways to transport Bibles into Romania
and the former Soviet Union
194 pages $11.99

A Heart to Belong / *by Johnny Miller*
A Heart to Belong (sequel to HeartBridge) continues the story of
God's sustaining grace as the Millers love and guide the children of the
Nathaniel Christian Orphanage in Romania.
302 pages $12.99

THE WAY TO GOD AND PEACE

We live in a world contaminated by sin. Sin is anything that goes against God's holy standards. When we do not follow the guidelines that God our Creator gave us, we are guilty of sin. Sin separates us from God, the source of life.

Since the time when the first man and woman, Adam and Eve, sinned in the Garden of Eden, sin has been universal. The Bible says that we all have "sinned and come short of the glory of God" (Romans 3:23). It also says that the natural consequence for that sin is eternal death, or punishment in an eternal hell: "Then when lust hath conceived, it bringeth forth sin: and sin, when it is finished, bringeth forth death" (James 1:15).

But we do not have to suffer eternal death in hell. God provided forgiveness for our sins through the death of His only Son, Jesus Christ. Because Jesus was perfect and without sin, He could die in our place. "For God so loved the world that he gave his only begotten Son, that whosoever believeth in him should not perish, but have everlasting life" (John 3:16).

A sacrifice is something given to benefit someone else. It costs the giver greatly. Jesus was God's sacrifice. Jesus' death takes away the penalty of sin for everyone who accepts this sacrifice and truly repents of their sins. To repent of sins means to be truly sorry for and turn away from the things we have done that have violated God's standards. (Acts 2:38; 3:19).

Jesus died, but He did not remain dead. After three days, God's Spirit miraculously raised Him to life again. God's Spirit does something similar in us. When we receive Jesus as our sacrifice and repent of our sins, our hearts are changed. We become spiritually alive! We develop new desires and attitudes (2 Corinthians 5:17). We begin to make choices that please God (1 John 3:9). If we do fail and commit sins, we can ask God for forgiveness. "If we confess our sins, he is faithful and just to forgive us our sins, and to cleanse us from all unrighteousness" (1 John 1:9).

Once our hearts have been changed, we want to continue growing spiritually. We will be happy to let Jesus be the Master of our lives and will want to become more like Him. To do this, we must meditate on God's Word and commune with God in prayer. We will testify to others of this change by being baptized and sharing the good news of God's victory over sin and death. Fellowship with a faithful group of believers will strengthen our walk with God (1 John 1:7).